SHINE
UNTIL TOMORROW

D1558840

Text copyright © 2024 Leia M. Johnson

First published in 2024 by Phoenix Media & Books, LLC
PO Box 1151, O'Fallon, IL 62269
www.phoenixmediaandbooks.com

All rights reserved

No part of this publication may be reproduced,
distributed, or transmitted in any form or by any means,
including photocopying, recording, or other electronic
or mechanical methods, without the prior written permission
of the publisher, except as permitted by U.S. copyright law.

Book cover designed by April Marciszewski
Artwork by Marcel Marciszewski
Book interior design and typesetting by Larry Issa
Edited by Katie Otey, Nancy Hollingsworth, Jamie Holaday

Library of Congress Control Number: on file with publisher
Print ISBN: 978-1-7361303-6-0
E-Book ISBN: 978-1-7361303-8-4

SHINE
UNTIL TOMORROW

Navigating Paradigm Shifts
When Life Doesn't Meet Expectations

a memoir

LEIA M. JOHNSON

PHOENIX MEDIA & BOOKS

For Kelly, Teagan, and Amber—
my village, my polo-a-friend lifelines, my mafia

And for all the kids who deserve better

AUTHOR'S NOTE

This is my story, but it's impossible to tell without also telling the stories of other people. I agree in general with Anne Lamott who said in her book, *Bird by Bird*, "You own everything that happened to you. Tell your stories. If people wanted you to write warmly about them, they should have behaved better." But I also acknowledge the sticky power dynamic involved in being an adoptive parent talking about my children's first parents.

Anything negative I felt or feel about the people discussed in these pages is not a result of them doing something directly to me, but rather a complicated process of working out a relationship dynamic that is new to all of us. Also, at the risk of telling too much of the story up front, I believe the relationships I have with these people can withstand the tension this storytelling may create. We have treated each other with a mutual and kind candor for years, and nothing here will come as a surprise to any of them.

In discussing the details of the case, I've tried to focus more on how certain factors affected me versus guessing about thoughts and feelings of other people involved. There are many sides to every story, and I've told my truth while attempting to extend grace and empathy to all the players who might remember things differently. If I have failed anywhere to respect the humanity of the people involved, I sincerely apologize.

Throughout the book, I've sprinkled snippets from social media and blog posts I wrote to provide context for some of what was happening in "real time." I debated keeping these, but early readers agreed that they provided some comedic relief that serves as respite from the heaviness of the rest of the story. Combing through my Facebook and Instagram posts for some of these lighter moments also gave me a cathartic reminder that while this time of life was full of pain, the day to day raising of these children was full of immense joy.

Out of respect for all parties, some details of this story fall into a category of "not my story to tell." One metric I used in deciding to keep some more shocking or negative information in the manuscript was if the details are a matter of verifiable public record. Also, due to the nature of some of the sensitive information, some adult names have been changed.

One of the more difficult challenges I faced is wrestling with how to tell the parts of this story that involve minors in a way that honors a level of consent that they are not yet old enough to give. Regarding medical information, I have included details that are common to kids in foster care and thus hopefully instructive in nature. Nothing here is meant to satisfy the desires of voyeur-tourists. Also, any details included would never be a surprise to my girls as we have shared these stories in age-appropriate ways and will continue to do so as they get older.

The ethics of storytelling are as murky as the ethics of adoption, and I continue to fight in both of these arenas for a world that honors all parties involved. I hope this book offers a path to a nuanced conversation that is much bigger than any missteps I may have made in writing this manuscript. I welcome feedback that is intended to help me grow in my thinking.

INTRODUCTION

Over the course of twelve stolen Mondays with the aid of 36 cups of coffee at five rickety café tables, I finished the first draft of this book. I say the Mondays were stolen because my life as a military spouse and mother of four demands that I become a time alchemist, creating hours in my day that aren't there. The truth is there is no magic involved. I have the same number of hours as every other human, and writing anything requires me to steal time from countless competing priorities.

For six Mondays in the spring of 2019, my saintly mom committed to covering my kids, so I could have uninterrupted writing time. That summer, we uprooted from the cornfields of southern Illinois and replanted ourselves in the damp evergreen woods of Olympia, Washington. The business of starting a new life in a new town—finding doctors, dentists, and therapists; enrolling four kids in school; unpacking a house; and starting a new job consumed the fall and early winter. Then I found six more Mondays in the first two cold, dark months of 2020 to finish the manuscript.

We all know what happened in February and March of 2020. Every one of us found ourselves reconfiguring our lives from top to bottom. For me, that meant teaching my class of wiggly preschoolers through Zoom, while also coming up with a plan for the four kids pandemic-schooling from the comfort of our dining room. We created a work-from-home space in a cramped corner of the guest bedroom for my husband, Scott, a squadron commander in the Air Force. As the Reverend Tim Gunn says, we made it work.

Any momentum I had created in pursuing publication died with the old normal, and I found myself staring longingly at the writing folder of my Google drive knowing I would eventually come up for breath and steal some more hours. What I didn't know at the beginning of the pandemic was that the time my manuscript spent collecting dust on the bottom shelf of my life was a growing season—for me, for our family, and for the manuscript. If I had picked it back up during that time of frustrated longing, I would have published the wrong book.

━━

Since childhood, Alice from Wonderland has always been one of my favorite characters. I love the scene in the Disney adaptation when Alice, consumed by an existential crisis after shrinking to three inches in height meets a hookah-smoking, grammar-obsessed caterpillar. Alice grows frustrated by the caterpillar's riddles. As he transforms into a butterfly and flies away, the caterpillar offers Alice one helpful hint: her destiny relies upon which side of the mushroom she chooses to eat—one side will make her shrink, and one side will make her grow.

If anything, the pandemic disrupted my well-thought-out plans and brought into intense focus the "mushrooms" in my life, those moments that have the potential to help me shrink or grow depending on my choices. Fungi, while potentially dangerous, play an important role in our ecosystem. They decompose what needs to be destroyed, and they aid in new growth of plants. As agents of fermentation, they make some foods edible. Fungi have been used to create life-saving antibiotics. And the thing I love most about mushrooms? They grow in dark, damp spaces where very few life forms would be able to thrive.

Yes, this is the story of how our family came to be. It's a story about military life and about foster care and adoption. But more importantly, this is a story about choosing the narrow path over the wide road and about what happens when our expectations don't match reality. While I and others have written many stories about looking for the light, this is a story about when growth happens in dark spaces.

I hope you find a companion to your own story in these pages, and that yours is a pilgrimage to love and meaning like mine. Thank you for reading.

CHAPTER 1

The Call

The afternoon I received The Call was typical of most midwestern December days. The highs all week had been in the 40s, but the cloudless sky and bright sunshine were enough to make the boys halfheartedly complain when I suggested they wear hats and gloves on our morning walk to school. At eleven and eight, both Will and Ben were growing into their independence, and I was settling into a new level of complementary freedom. They could legitimately feed, clothe, and clean themselves and only required the occasional loving nudge to brush their teeth or to be in bed on time.

I ran some errands before afternoon pick up and then pulled into the parking lot of the boys' school with about five minutes to spare. As I scrolled through Facebook, my phone rang. It was Carolyn, our licensing worker. After taking the requisite classes and completing a home study through a social services agency, we had received our foster care license in the mail five days before. Carolyn was calling to schedule our quarterly meeting—she wanted to know if Friday would work, and I consulted the calendar on my phone to confirm.

"How's 9:00?" I asked.

"That's fine," Carolyn answered, her voice muffled as if she was balancing the phone on her shoulder while trying to do something else.

"We have a three-month-old baby girl in the office. Do you think you could take her?"

Record scratch.

I was sure I had misunderstood because she said it so nonchalantly. This was a phone call about a routine meeting. In my mind, I had expected doves to fly out of the phone while the Mormon Tabernacle Choir sang the "Hallelujah Chorus" when we got The Call. Carolyn was … making conversation.

I took a breath and said, "What do you know about her?"

Carolyn yawned a bit and said, "Ooooh, excuse me. I need a nap. We think she is about three months old. She's white. No major issues that we know about at the moment."

"Let me see if I can get ahold of Scott at work to confirm," I said. "But I think we can do that. I'll call you back."

"Okay, I'll put you down as a maybe," Carolyn said. "Other workers are making calls, too. Call me back as soon as you can, so I can tell them she's been placed."

"Sure thing. Talk to you in a bit." I hung up. Will and Ben came bounding out of the building toward me. I noticed their hats and gloves had been abandoned and hoped everything had made it back into their backpacks. As I helped them into the car, I could feel cold sweat gathering in my armpits. *Is this really happening?* I took a deep calming breath and made sure the side doors of the minivan were shut and everyone was buckled in before pulling out of my parking space to head home. *A baby a baby a baby a baby a baby.* A bit dazedly I asked, "How was your day, guys?"

The boys rushed to talk over one another—one telling me he didn't have any homework and one relating a story about a joke he told in class. Meanwhile, I dialed Scott's work number. An Air Force pilot by trade, Scott was the reason we were living in southern Illinois. For this assignment, he was "flying" a desk instead of flying cargo planes around the world. When he answered, I blurted out what I knew and waited for him to respond.

"Wow—a three-month-old?" he paused. "I mean … this is what we signed up for, right?"

"Yeah, I guess so," I said. But honestly, it was yes and no. In all of our classes, they talked about the need for people to be available for older children. We had committed to taking kids younger than our boys, but that still left a window up to eight years of age. I think we both thought we would get a call for an older child. But a baby? I knew Scott was likely thinking similar thoughts.

"What do I need to do?" Scott asked. "Should I come home?"

It was 3:15—fifteen minutes after Carolyn's call had come through. His work day typically ended around 4:30. My heart was beating out of my chest, but my brain was in strategy mode. "No, I don't think you need to come home. I'll tell Carolyn we'll take the baby unless someone else already has."

When I hung up the phone with Scott, I explained what was happening to the boys. They were excited, but they were more concerned that our first placement wouldn't be able to play video games with them.

When I called Carolyn back, I'd had enough time to mentally prepare some questions. *What was her name? Were there any medical issues? Were there signs of abuse or neglect? Why was she removed from the home? Did she have siblings?* Our second conversation was brief. She didn't know much more beyond the baby's name. Carolyn said the worker who would transport her would give me more information, and she would be on her way shortly.

"Shortly? Can you give me a timeframe?" I asked.

"We're gathering some things here at the office, and then she will drive over," Carolyn said. The office was seven minutes from our house, and it was almost 4:00.

At 4:20, a middle-aged woman named Erica dropped a three-month-old baby named Emma at my house. She told me that Emma had a sister that was placed with a relative, and someone would be by Thursday to pick the baby up for visitation with her dad. A caseworker would complete an initial shopping trip in the next week for basic supplies. They would call me with the details later. And then Erica left.

Will, Ben, and I stared at the baby sleeping soundly in her car seat. I lifted her out, thinking she was the teeniest thing I'd ever seen. We found out later that she weighed ten pounds and was considered "failure to thrive." She was swimming in gray and purple pajamas. She had cradle cap that covered the top of her head and spread down her forehead to her eyebrows. She smelled like cigarette smoke.

The boys and I took turns holding her, remarking how her ears seemed too big for her tiny head and her nose looked like Tinker Bell's. She had a mess of dark hair, worn thin in the back from lying flat. Her head was turned to the right, her neck stuck in a twisted position.

She was perfect.

When I say she was perfect, I mean that within minutes of meeting Emma, I knew that I would give her my whole heart for as long as she needed it. This is the great fear of foster care—the thing people obsess about most. *What if I get attached?*

Well, what if you do? I did. She did. We all did. Because human beings are meant to connect. The night Emma came to live with us was a test, not just for foster care but for a life well-lived.

For over a decade, the Air Force had provided plenty of opportunities for us to love people and say goodbye. That is the nature of our lifestyle. It is heartbreaking to leave places and people we love, but it is our duty and privilege, and our family is made for this. We fall in love fast and hard despite knowing we will someday wave in the rearview mirror. The alternative is to stay disconnected, and that is no way to live.

When foster care became real in the form of an underweight baby girl, we were ready to answer the call of loving a child for as long as she needed us. We thought we knew what that meant, but we had so much more to learn.

CHAPTER TWO
The Baby

Somewhere in the middle of figuring all of this out, I'd told Scott to go to his regular Crossfit class. When I said those words, there was no reason for him to rush home early. I wasn't even sure the baby was coming to our house, and if she was, surely he had time to work out before she arrived. Insert all the laughs.

The first time Scott met Emma, he barely had time to give her a good once over while wearing sweaty workout clothes and shuffling the boys out the door for karate. All too quickly, I found myself alone in the house with this tiny stranger who didn't make a sound. In the hour and forty minutes she had been in our house, she hadn't moved or opened her eyes. I knew she'd spent the majority of the day being shuffled around in cars and then hanging out in the case manager's office, so it made sense that she was tired.

Erica had dropped Emma off with two cans of formula, telling me that someone had fed her in the office right before they came to our house. She had a bag with a picture of Tweety Bird and the name "Taylor" stitched across it, which contained a few mismatched items of clothing, four diapers, and a bottle. Because I'd breastfed exclusively, I had to read the instructions on the can to feed her. A week would pass before the case manager would complete the shopping trip, so I started a list of essentials to buy at the store the next day.

As I sat (not) alone in the house, my friend, Megan, came to mind. At a book club meeting a month before, she had offered some baby hand-me-downs should we ever need them, so I texted her letting her know Emma had arrived. While Scott and the boys were at karate, Megan showed up with a baby bath, a playmat, a bouncy seat, a mountain of burp cloths, and a few other odds and ends. I remember pulling out the burp cloths later and thinking, *"Burp cloths! I forgot about those!"*

My kids were in fifth and second grade. I had forgotten so much. I was genuinely excited to have a baby in the house and equally baffled by my inability to remember things like how much a three month old should weigh or eat or sleep. What was she supposed to be doing developmentally?

During our foster care training and in the years since, my mission to become more informed has led me to explore the work of prominent child psychologists and neuroscientists. Groundbreaking work at the Karyn Purvis Institute of Child Development at Texas Christian University informs us of the effects of trauma on "children from hard places." Through the work of Dr. Purvis and her colleagues, we are learning more and more about how children survive trauma. I tried to wake Emma up to feed her an inexpertly made bottle, and she ate but stayed asleep the entire time. Later, as I began to learn more about in utero and infant trauma, I came to understand what happened for the first two weeks that she was in our home.

Emma was born over a month early and exposed to prolonged nicotine and cocaine use while in utero. For nearly three months before she came to our house, she lived in unclean conditions with active drug use and smoking in the home. We were advised by foster care professionals that the probable reason for her sleeping around the clock was infant depression related to both her in utero and postnatal experiences. I had never heard the term "infant depression" and had a hard time wrapping my mind around the concept. We were told it was crucial for her to build strong attachments to her caregivers in order to get her back on track. We learned that in utero drug use can cause both plagiocephaly (her flat head) and torticollis (her twisted neck). Her physical therapists recommended she come three times a week for six months to address this. They believed she would need to wear a helmet for a year.

In those early weeks, I don't know that I allowed myself to process any feelings about all of Emma's conditions. I was too busy with the daily work of caring for three children. The first week she was with us, I got to work getting rid of her cradle cap. I'd seen cradle cap on both of my boys, but it was short-lived and minor. Emma's cradle cap was layered and extensive. For three nights in a row, I treated her head with jojoba oil mixed with geranium and lavender. After these moisturizing treatments, I combed out the flaky skin with a tiny comb and rinsed her under a warm bath.

She was most awake during bathtime and started making noise for the first time when she was lying in her tub. As I poured warm water over her head each night, she cooed, and I noticed how the high-calorie formula the pediatrician had recommended was filling out the wrinkles in her scrawny legs. Her face, all angles and points the night she arrived, was starting to take shape—round with a dimple on one cheek. When we returned for her ten-day check up after being placed in our home, she had gained one pound and fourteen ounces. Along with her doctor and nurses, I stood next to the scale and cheered.

As Emma began to "wake up" more and more, we would often lay her on a blanket, positioning ourselves to her left, so she was forced to turn her head to see and hear us better. We worked hard on her therapies at home—the boys loved helping massage her head and neck. We sang "Let's Get Physical!" while we did her baby workouts. After three weeks of physical therapy, we were released with instructions to follow up with her pediatrician. She would not need a helmet. We were told to continue doing exactly what we were doing at home, and we were proud that our hard work was paying off.

When I shared news of the progress with our circle of support, I didn't talk about how quickly I was starting to resent Emma's caregivers who had allowed this to happen because I wasn't ready to process those feelings with others. While we were so happy with the numbers on her charts, I was up at night crying. I cried angry tears of disgust about why a baby was subjected to this. I cried hopeless tears for all the babies in the world enduring similar injustices. We had been a foster family for less than a month, and every morning brought a stiff resolve to right this wrong. That determination kept me from being overwhelmed by the big picture. Minute by minute, hour by hour, we were fulfilling our commitment to the state of Illinois to care for this baby until her parents could get her back.

It was at the ten-day check-up that I had the opportunity to meet Emma's birth mom, Jessica. I had some jitters because I was working on limited information about who she was. I had created a caricature based on the snippets I'd gathered from the case manager. I had asked questions that were met with "I can't tell you that" or "I don't know" more often than not. I knew Jessica was twenty and had just given birth to her fourth child. I knew Emma and her sister were brought into care following a domestic dispute.

I also knew that before the girls were brought into care, Jessica was part of an "intact" case. In the state of Illinois, investigators will often allow mothers to take children home from the hospital with the caveat that they must check in with an intact worker. In theory, this gives the mother a chance to bond with her baby and keeps the baby from being placed in foster care. With added support, many of these moms are able to get the resources they need to care for their children. The intent is to make sure that only the most extreme cases warrant foster care.

To say I had and still have mixed feelings about this is an understatement. The decision about whether or not a baby comes into care is left up to the investigator. Investigators are human, so they are bound to make mistakes on tough calls. Take this hypothetical (but realistic) situation—a sixteen-year-old girl gives birth to her first baby. The investigator notes that she has a history of drug or alcohol abuse and is living at home with her parents. He decides to funnel that young mother to an intact case. She is required to submit to drug tests, parenting classes, and regular visits from her worker. If she is meeting minimal parenting standards, and her baby is doing well after a period of time, her case will be closed. That is how an intact case works to the benefit of young, struggling mothers.

In our case, Emma was drug exposed and born a month early to a twenty-year-old mother with three other children. There were several other red flags that led me to question how on earth this baby had been allowed to go home from the hospital. While my thoughts and feelings about many things in our case have evolved over time, this is one piece of information that continues to baffle me. I firmly believe that sending Emma home with Jessica from the hospital was the wrong call. That decision led to three months of a baby suffering unnecessarily and an unfair burden on a mother who was suffering her own trauma. I'm also aware that it's much easier for me to assess the situation in hindsight.

Biological parents are encouraged to attend doctor's appointments while their kids are in care. I was eager to put a face with a name because, without knowing Jessica, it was easy to judge her poor choices. I anticipated her being standoffish—after all, I was a stranger taking care of her baby. Illinois had taken Emma into care, but it's hard to be mad at The State. I understood that I might be the face of Jessica's greatest struggle. In an effort to build a bridge, I printed some pictures to put in a photo album from the short time Emma had been with us. As nervous as I was about meeting Jessica, I'm sure my discomfort paled in comparison to how she was feeling about meeting me.

The first time I saw her, I kept staring because although her clothes were torn and her makeup smudged, I couldn't get over how pretty she was. She was thin, and her hair had been dyed multiple colors at different times. She looked tired, but to my surprise, she wasn't hostile or rude or outwardly angry. Instead, she took Emma out of her carseat and stared at her. She made comments about how big she looked. She'd grown so much in just a few days. She snapped some pictures of the baby with her phone, and I handed her the photo album I'd put together.

While we waited for the doctor, we chatted about what kind of progress Emma was making. Jessica asked questions about our family and seemed relieved to know that the family taking care of her child was a good one. While I had a laundry list of questions floating around in my brain, I didn't want to seem nosy or overbearing, so I tried to let her lead the conversation. I noticed a giant, partially healed scar on her forearm. She saw me notice. Wide-eyed, she said, "I punched out a window."

I can't speak to her intent, but on my end it felt like she was trying to communicate how tough she was, like she was proud of the scar. She stared at me, and I let a beat pass before responding that it looked like the wound was healing. She added that she was injured the night the girls were put in foster care.

This was our first placement, but based on stories I'd heard from friends and in training, I was prepared for the worst. Most of the narratives I've heard about foster parents and biological parents are riddled with tension. Either biological parents are hateful or dangerous, foster parents are not open to a relationship with biological parents, or both. I think biological parents often think that foster parents have more power to control things than they actually do. Out of a combination of life experiences (or lack thereof), assumptions, and protective instincts, foster parents can paint biological parents with a broad negative brush.

None of this is helpful.

Scott and I have always been good at resolving conflict. One of the things we try to keep at the center of our marriage is that we're on the same team. This extends to conflicts that arise with our boys. When someone is frustrated and lashing out, it is common for someone else to shout "SAME TEAM!"

Because it's easy to forget. We might not agree. We might be so mad at each other that we can't think rationally, but we're a family that wants the same things at the end of the day. It followed pretty naturally that we would extend this "same team" mentality into the world of foster care.

In that first meeting with Jessica, I tried my best to communicate with her that my goal wasn't to keep her baby—quite the opposite actually. I was here to cheer her on as she worked her service plan and got her kids back. I couldn't control a lot of the process. In fact, ten days into a case that would eventually take more than two and a half years to find permanency, I felt like I was running around a dark maze bumping into walls most of the time.

More than anything, I needed her to know that my role in this was not to decide what was required of her. It was not to decide whether she was a fit parent. My job was to care for the baby placed in my home by the state of Illinois. I promised her that I would do my best to care for Emma, and Jessica needed to know that we were on her team.

Looking back, I recognize a bit of naivete on my part—a combination of my general take-charge approach to life and my innate belief that human beings are good. I believed that if I remained open and vulnerable and self-aware, I would be able to influence others to do the same, and in the end, we would accomplish our goals of protecting children, contributing to a care team, and mentoring parents who needed extra support. The longer our case wore on and the deeper we got into the labyrinth of the system, the more I realized how difficult this would be.

Blog Post: January 6, 2017
There is time for the feelings to be processed, and we have such an incredible network of support in our friends and family. We don't know what will happen, and we have no way to control any of it, but I will tell you that this feels like the holiest work I've ever done.

CHAPTER THREE
The Visits

Two weeks after Emma arrived, we had a trip planned to Missouri and Oklahoma to visit friends and family for Christmas, and after filling out some travel consents, Emma was free to go with us. My extended family is large, and like countless times in my life, we gathered at someone's house to eat a meal and open presents. At one of our stops, we huddled in one room—grandparents, cousins, aunts and uncles—and set the timer on the camera to capture all twenty-seven people, including one tiny, sleepy baby wrapped in my mom's arms, her face shielded from view. In choosing to share our story on social media, I had to get creative because in the state of Illinois, the faces of children identified as being in care cannot be shown online. All of the early pictures we shared of Emma were of her tiny toes, the rolls forming on her thighs, and the back of her head which was rounding out nicely.

On Christmas Eve, we drove to Oklahoma, arriving in time to have Christmas Eve dinner at a Mexican restaurant with Scott's family and friends, a long-standing tradition. Emma snoozed in her carrier while I filled everyone in on updates about the case and tried not to drop salsa on her. That night, we hung out at Scott's mom's house, snacking on Woody's toffee and chatting about Thunder basketball. At one point,

Emma started crying, which was uncharacteristic of her despite the fact that she was almost four months old. We took turns holding her, and nothing helped. We determined she had gas when her cry became screams and she pulled her legs into her belly. I know this sounds odd because babies cry, but we were all shocked at the noises she was making. Our baby was upset in a way we'd never seen before.

Scott grabbed some gas drops out of the diaper bag, and she took them angrily while I positioned her on my shoulder hoping it would help the gas pass. All of the adults talked over each other, questioning if it was just gas or something more, and I noticed the boys standing a few feet away, both of them staring intently with looks of concern on their faces. Will had tears streaming down his face.

"Oh, buddy. Come here," I said, offering my free arm to embrace him. I stood with one tiny baby on my left shoulder, and the head of my biggest baby on my right. "What's wrong?"

Through muffled sobs, I heard him say, "I don't want her to be in pain."

I assured him it was just gas and that once the drops were in her system a little longer, she would be fine. I motioned for Ben to join us in our group hug and told both of them I loved them. They were such good big brothers. Within minutes, she calmed down and started smiling. All was calm. All was bright.

Over the next few days, everywhere we went someone had pajamas or a rattle or some other baby necessity for Emma. When we decided to foster, I thought about what that meant to everyone in our immediate circle. Their thoughtfulness and the way they loved her while also asking, "How long will she be with you?" spoke volumes. Three weeks into being a foster family, our people were telling us, "We don't understand this, but we're here." We traveled back to Illinois feeling refreshed and refueled for what lay ahead.

Sometime in the beginning of January, the judge set a visitation schedule. Emma was to leave our house every weekday for four hours a day. A case assistant would pick her up on Monday, Tuesday, and Friday to visit her mom. Another case assistant would pick her up on Wednesday and Thursday to visit her dad, Chad. At this point, she'd lived with us for about a month, and it was impossible to remain an impartial caregiver despite my rational self-talk. There was just no way our family was going to spend our waking hours meeting this baby's basic needs without falling head over heels in love with her.

No amount of training or listening to other people's stories could have prepared me for the level of emotional conflict I would experience as I tried to sift through my prescribed role in this world and the natural tendency to love. As a foster parent, I followed the mandate of providing a safe, stable environment and temporary home for kids in crisis. There are easy-to-follow unwritten rules that serve as guidance—show your kids in care how to love, teach them how to care for their bodies and minds, help them learn to self-regulate.

We had no idea if she would leave after six weeks or six months. She might have moved to another foster home if the case manager felt it was the right thing to do. A family member might have shown up willing to care for her. She might have lived with us for two years and then gone home to her first parents. At that point, there was no way to know. This kind of uncertainty is at the core of what foster care means. This is the reason foster care exists.

By design, when regular visitation began, I had no say in when or where those visits took place. Some places were ruled out for safety issues, but otherwise, the visits were scheduled to accommodate her parents' schedules and requests. Intellectually, I understood that measures were in place to keep Emma safe when she left our home, but my heart still felt heavy every time our case assistant, Michelle, walked out the door with "our" baby. I know. She wasn't *ours*. But she was.

Other foster parents gave me the advice to keep notes on anything that impacted Emma's case. I started logging relevant information. I kept track of how many of these visits occurred and how long they lasted. Often, the case assistant would pick her up, drive her to the visit, and return home within the hour because a parent did not show up or something happened to end the visit. We had limited knowledge about why the visits ended. Many times, the case assistant would call half an hour before the visit was scheduled and tell me the visit was canceled. Again, I often had no idea why.

A couple of times, when I pressed the issue, the case assistant would tell me something like, "We arrived and no one answered the door, so I stayed the required fifteen minutes and brought her back to you." I never worried about her when she went to her dad's house. She always came back clean, fed, and diapered. She occasionally smelled faintly of smoke but usually it was evident that she was cared for when visiting his home. Sometimes she even came home with little gifts—a new pair of shoes or a stuffed animal. We found out at a permanency hearing six months later that Chad was sleeping through many of his visits because he worked late nights, and his girlfriend, whose name was on the Tweety Bird bag that came with Emma that first night, was caring for her instead.

Without knowing what was happening during these visits, I was relieved and impressed every time she came back to us with a fresh diaper and having been fed. Taylor even washed out the bottles after feeding her and sent a message through the case assistant about how many ounces she'd eaten.

Emma's visits with her mom, on the other hand, were erratic, sporadic, and unpredictable. For those first few weeks, the visits were canceled more than they happened, and when Jessica did make a visit, they ended early. Planning anything in my day was challenging to say the least. My parents were permanently on call. I generally gave myself a minute to throw an internal hissy fit about the inconvenience and then pep talked my way back to a good attitude. *This is what you signed up for. You cannot control any of this. Support the plan. Be grateful that Emma is back "home."*

In my less than gracious moments, I spent a lot of time screaming about how no one cared about the children involved. Poor Scott sat across the room nodding his head during countless tirades about how many resources—human and otherwise—were being wasted on these parents who didn't have the decency to show up for a visit with their children. I was not keeping a "same team" mentality. I had a "screw the team, the manager, and the owner" mentality. At certain points in the process, I practically tried to burn down the clubhouse and the whole stadium. NOT THE SAME TEAM. I did not want to be on the same team anymore when I felt like I was the only player showing up for the game.

Some of my frustration was directed at Emma's biological parents, and I'm not proud of any of the judgmental thoughts I had about them. Most of my frustration was with the decisions the caseworker and other people in the system made that did not seem to benefit the children in any way. Again and again, I was offered the "policy and procedure" party line for why we were waking babies up from naps and dragging them out in the cold for visits we all knew weren't going to happen.

I am someone who believes in second chances. Honestly, I believe in third and fourth and fifth chances most of the time. However, it was hard to feel magnanimous about giving extra chances when Emma was affected in directly negative ways because adults weren't using common sense. This is the part of foster care that makes foster parents quit. I knew we would encounter difficult people. I knew we would be navigating trauma. I knew my foster parent rights and responsibilities like the back of my hand. I knew there would be daily frustration and heartache. What I could never have understood until I was actually living it was the number of times I would raise a legitimate concern about the welfare of the child in my care and be told my concerns were not valid.

For example, I texted the case assistant one day and asked if we could move the visit to thirty minutes later. Emma had been up all night with an ear infection, and I'd finally gotten her down for a nap. She wasn't running a high enough fever to cancel the visit altogether, but

I thought she could really benefit from finishing her nap. Thirty minutes would be ample time to make this happen. I had never made any requests like this before, but I felt like this one would best serve the sick baby. The case assistant was brand new, so she texted back that the visit could not be moved. When I pushed back, she said she would have her supervisor call me.

The supervisor called and said the visit could not be changed, and if I didn't comply, I could potentially be held accountable in court. This was her reaction out of the gate—no clarifying questions, no room for me to explain my reasoning. And the mention of court? Not only was that patently false because foster parents aren't on trial, but the comment was a veiled threat by someone asserting authority in a completely inappropriate manner. This was the first instance I experienced of someone acting like I was somehow doing something wrong and needed to be put in my place. I had never met this person, and she treated me as disrespectfully as I've ever been treated in my life.

When I tried to explain, she talked over me. When I raised my voice because she wouldn't allow me to get a sentence out, she yelled back that our conversation was over and hung up. Honestly, I spent the time between the phone call and when the case assistant showed up to take Emma to her visit crying and trying to calm down. I put Emma into her car seat and watched as the case assistant loaded her into the car. They were back within the hour because her mom did not show.

My objections were not just about the baby. So much of the process did not serve the parents either. For instance, if a parent misses a certain number of visits in a row, it makes sense that visits would be suspended until the caseworker could meet with the parent to discuss needed adjustments. I believed Jessica was being held to an unfair standard from the beginning, and she was never able to build momentum. Making three visits for a total of twelve hours a week was too much to ask a twenty-year-old mother of four who was also supposed to be finding a stable living situation, getting a job, and completing a service plan that included hours of classes and counseling sessions. Jessica didn't have an ID, a high school diploma, or means of transportation other than the bus. Asking someone in her darkest hour, not to mention the lifelong trauma that led her to this moment, to have this kind of time management is absurd.

What was even more baffling is that the things that seemed important—requiring parents to find a ride to the visit and to provide necessary supplies like diapers and formula ranked low on the priority list. These basic requirements were waived over and over. The message was that no one *really* expected Jessica to cover even the small stuff. Instead of cutting her required hours and holding her to basic standards, we watched her fail to meet her visit requirements, losing steam quickly with each failure and then disappearing completely for weeks at a time. I recognize that parents have to be held to a standard of personal responsibility, but the way the current system is devised offers a mountain of expectations with limited, erratic support. Early on, I tried to offer help, but when the entire tone is set by a system that feels adversarial, it is difficult to build trust with anyone involved.

I have said over and over again that case managers have the hardest job in the world. They are overworked, underpaid, and underappreciated. One of the biggest challenges is figuring out how to make smart choices for the kids in care while treating parents fairly. In a perfect world, the "team" would be communicating regularly about how to move forward in a way that benefits both the kids and their biological parents, but reality often looks like case managers spinning their wheels to make a difference while getting slammed by the system's rules and abused by angry parents.

It's easy to point fingers at everyone in these scenarios to highlight all the things they did wrong. The parents didn't show up. The caseworker didn't communicate. The foster parent didn't cooperate. Tempers flare. Feelings get hurt. Everyone is tired. All of the frustrations and tension taught me the importance of not judging people by the worst thing you know or think about them.

I learned to funnel my anger into productivity as best as I could, and every time I was frustrated because people at our agency pushed back or Emma's parents failed to care for her well, I became more resolved to be her advocate. On my best days, I recognized that everyone involved was spinning a lot of plates, and Emma was one of their plates.

I would not make this baby a plate. She deserved better—she was a human, flesh and blood, not a name on a form, and not a bullet point on a list of priorities. If those early frustrations taught me anything, it was to keep Emma in the center of everything I did. I would not waste energy on being mad about things that inconvenienced me or irritations about the case manager or biological parents. I resolved to put the full force of my efforts behind making sure Emma was not a victim of further injustice. What I learned was that saving my energy for the things that really mattered brought the rest of my life into intense focus as well.

Instead of focusing on everything I couldn't control, I started celebrating every little victory. The boys were doing well in school despite all the changes. Victory. My parents were the pillars holding up our family in the storm. Victory. We took Emma to her four-month well-child check, and in six weeks, she'd gone from failure to thrive and multiple diagnoses to being in the 50th percentile for height and weight and in no need of physical therapy. Huge victory.

Facebook: February 8, 2017
Today at lunch, when the day was not going as planned …
Me: I hate everyone.
Scott: I like you.
Ladies and gentlemen, this is why we are still married.
#luckiest #marriagemasterclass

CHAPTER FOUR
The Toddler

During the first couple months of 2017, we met Faith, Emma's older sister. Faith was initially placed with a relative from her first dad's side of the family at the same time Emma was placed with us. When the case assistant picked Emma up for visits with Jessica, Faith was in the car as well. Several times, I noted that she was dirty and inadequately dressed for the winter weather. Still, she seemed to be happy, saying "Hi!" anytime I stuck my head in the van while putting Emma in her car seat. At the beginning of February, the case manager expressed some concerns about Faith's well being. Her relative caregiver was young and taking care of three other children. The case manager felt like the caregiver was overwhelmed, but there wasn't a significant reason to remove Faith from the home.

That changed when she showed up to a visit running a fever of over 103°. She had not seen a doctor. The case assistant called to let me know she would be bringing Emma home early because she didn't want her exposed, and Jessica would take Faith to urgent care during the remainder of the visit. That night, the case manager called stating that she had talked with Jessica about removing Faith from her relative caregiver based on medical neglect. Faith had been running a high fever for days, had a double ear infection, and had a rash from her belly button to her knees. Jessica said she thought it was a good idea to move Faith but only if she moved to our home. We did not have to think twice about accepting another placement.

Faith arrived at our house on Friday afternoon with everything the agency had supplied to her previous foster home. The case manager filled her prescriptions on the way to our house—three days after the doctor had ordered them. The case manager told us that the decision to move her was based on best practices for siblings to be together when possible and the fact that she had lost 10% of her body weight in the two months she had been in care. Everyone involved agreed that Jessica being on board with the move was a good sign because it meant she trusted us and appreciated the care we were giving Emma.

When Faith arrived, she was sick, dirty, and tired. The boys played with her while my parents and I put together her crib. At one point, she cried until she fell asleep on my dad's shoulder. We gave her a bath and found out that her matted, dishwater colored hair was curly and bright blonde. The first night she was with us, she ate two entire pieces of pizza and a pint of blueberries before we decided that was probably all her little stomach could handle. She was two days shy of eighteen months old.

When Faith came to live with us, we were told that she was developmentally delayed. The various therapists who had assessed her when she was brought into care had leveled her development at an average of about six to eight months younger than her actual age. At eighteen months, she had one word. She was underweight and recovering from compounded infections. We were told she would need tubes because she had basically had an ear infection for the last year of her life.

Because of her limited language skills, she communicated mostly by grunting and screaming. She threw things. She flailed on the ground, and the hardest part was that we never could predict what would trigger her rage. One day during the first week she was with us, we were trying to walk downstairs. She was carrying a cup of milk, a book, and a blanket. I reached down to take the cup as she was about to drop it. She threw everything out of her arms and nearly fell down the stairs, knocking me over in the process. Over her screams, I quickly realized that she was upset because I had taken the cup out of her hands. I calmly told her I was trying to help.

As she screamed "hi hi hi hi hi hi" over and over, she reached out for the cup that was now at the bottom of the stairs. I handed it back to her, and she calmed herself down with a drink. I sat next to her and asked if she wanted to sit in my lap. She let out a sigh of relief and started gathering her blanket and book. This time, I said, "Can I help you carry something? It looks like you have a lot in your arms." We locked eyes, something that didn't happen often. I watched her stand back up with her arms too full and start again on the stairs, sniffling as she went. This was a child who was very used to taking care of herself in ways no baby should ever know.

I cried so many times in those first couple of weeks with Faith, not because parenting a toddler is hard but because I realized I would never know how many times she'd been left to fend for herself. Every day, as her vocabulary improved and her cheeks chunked up, I also saw remnants of her mysterious past life—the way she hoarded food, the way she had no apparent attachment to anyone in particular or a sense of stranger danger appropriate for her age, the way she raged over every instance when she felt I was not trustworthy.

One thing we learned in training about trust-based relational intervention (TBRI) is that children who come from hard places often deal with hunger and food insecurity. Practitioners assert that all children benefit from having healthy snacks throughout the day, stating that best practices involve offering snacks every two hours to support blood sugar and to increase felt-safety. We took this advice to heart and created a "yes basket." The yes basket contained non-perishable food items like nuts, granola bars, and shelf-stable yogurt. The idea was that the basket was always accessible. The answer was always yes. We placed the basket at Faith's eye level in the pantry, so she knew she always had access to food.

In studying child development, I've learned again and again how healthy nutrition correlates directly with brain chemistry. Poor nutrition and chronic stress, two things from Faith's time before us, can disrupt neurotransmitters which are responsible for getting messages to our brains. Helping her feel secure about food and assisting in finding healthy choices was about more than parenting a toddler; it was about helping her brain heal. A few of the behaviors she was exhibiting regularly—aggression, anxiety, and fatigue—could be attributed to her chemistry being out of sorts. Of course, much of this is true for all toddlers, all people really, but her history demanded that we pay careful attention and be intentional about her healing.

Over time, we purposefully included Faith in shopping trips where she could pick snacks from the store shelves that appealed to her, giving her a sense of empowerment over her choices. Most importantly, I prepared for transitions by packing more snacks than anyone would ever think a toddler would need. I kept fruit snacks and Cheerios in the car. I carried an insulated bag with cheese and fruit to all of the boys' activities. At baseball games, I became everyone's favorite mom because all the little brothers and sisters knew they could come to me for food.

Perhaps even more important than food was Faith's access to water. Dehydration can cause drops in cognitive performance and lead to physical ailments. Our whole family drinks water well, so this wasn't a hard transition for us, but it was especially important to keep her hydrated. At the same time, Emma was learning to drink from a sippy cup, and both girls loved holding water bottles filled with ice.

Not only did this focus on hydration and nutrition serve Faith's physical needs in a tangible way, but it also served my mental health. So much of this process was completely out of my control, and the anxiety was ever present. Feelings of disappointment, sadness, and frustration simmered under the surface as I tried to remain a steadying force in her life. Learning about how to best serve her and then providing for her tangible needs were some of the only things I could control, which helped quell moments of overwhelm.

Facebook: February 21, 2017
Just today …
… I took both girls (reminder: 18 months and 5 months) to the store successfully for the first time.
… a teacher from the boys' school sent dinner home with my mom who was subbing today.
… my leggings guru sent me a package I ordered last week and snuck in a pair that are perfectly sized for our newest addition.
… a friend who sent a blanket for Baby E sent a matching one for sister F. Parts of the day were hard, but I can do hard things because so many people are helping me.
#fostercare #babygirls #sisters #yougetathankyou
#andyougetathankyou #everyonegetsathankyou

On top of feeling this immense responsibility to provide the first stability she'd ever known in her life, I became increasingly angry at the demands on our time—her time. As we were trying our best to help a toddler regulate with healthy food and regular bedtimes, we also had to send her out of the house for visits when she should have been napping, where she ate vending machine food and drank red Mountain Dew. We would celebrate developmental milestones or moments when we saw clear attachments forming, only to spend days recovering from these visits when her rage would bubble back up or her body rebelled with bouts of diarrhea and vomiting. We would make progress with her food issues, helping her feel safe and sure that she would always have access to food, only to see her regress into stuffing as much food into her mouth as she could until she threw up. The cycle was maddening.

In her book, *Falling Free*, Shannan Martin tells the story of how she and her husband built their family through adoption, eventually welcoming their grown adult son, Robert, a single teen father who had spent time in prison. When she speaks of the world their family entered by adopting Robert, she speaks of challenges most people would never even attempt to take on. There is one line in the book that became a mantra of sorts for me over time. She writes, "But when I tell you it was hard, I'm not done talking."

Three weeks after Faith was placed with us, therapists came to our house to reassess her developmental levels, something that is done every time a child is moved into a new foster home. They played with toys and talked to her. They asked some general questions about her routine and health. They filled out stacks of paperwork. After an hour in our home, the speech therapist spoke first. She told us that during that hour, they had recorded over 20 individual words Faith had used. The occupational therapist consulted her notebook and reported that in speech, fine motor, gross motor, and other measurable areas, F was measuring between 17–18 months. In other words, at 18 months and three weeks, she was well within normal range of development. In the coming months, her pediatrician would marvel at her healthy weight gain and tell us that she would not need tubes in her ears after all.

Again, there was no miracle strategy involved, only the blessed and tedious work of raising a baby. We gave her the medicine she needed. We fed her healthy food. We read her books. We gave her a bedtime in a comfortable bed. We rehearsed six words with her every night, and by the time she'd lived with us six weeks, she would proudly tell anyone who would listen: "I'm smart. I'm brave. I'm strong."

CHAPTER FIVE
The Adjusting

In two months' time, we doubled the number of children in our house. People sometimes ooh and aah over what feels like sacrifice and heroism to them, but I don't think any of us ever thought of this as exceptional. Taking two babies in as many months felt natural and normal and right. Even though this was our first direct experience with fostering, we knew that there was a great need for homes willing to take sibling groups. We shared the desire to keep these sisters together just like their caseworker and their biological mother. Their physical, psychological, and emotional challenges were problems to be solved, but loving and caring for these two tiny humans was easy.

In some ways, being an Air Force spouse prepared me for these challenges. For years, I had practiced smiling politely when people made frowny faces at me after finding out my husband was deployed. These looks of pity were almost always coupled with a "I don't know how you do it." Fostering brought another round of these conversations, and I kept smiling politely. How do any of us do anything, really? How do we do life?

My friend Kryste, better known as the Bossy Widow in our circle, lost her husband in a helicopter crash, leaving her with a house full of small children to wrangle alone. My friend Jana lost a baby days before his due date and then walked the halls of cancer wards with her next child before his fifth birthday. How did they do those things? Several years ago, I had the honor and privilege of climbing Mount Kilimanjaro to raise money for women living in war zones. During our time in the Democratic Republic of the Congo, I met women who were nursing children on their laps, almost all of whom were the product of violent rapes during decades-long conflict. How the hell do those women do it? And who am I to even compare my life to theirs?

I do *what* I do and *how* I do it because I am grateful for every single breath I have in my body. This life is more than so many people are afforded. I do what I do because as the great Mary Oliver says, I have been given "one wild and precious life," and I'm not going to waste it.

Once Faith was with us, we navigated sporadic visits with Jessica and even fewer visits for Emma with her dad, Chad. Faith's dad, Don, had not yet requested visits, so we had yet to incorporate that dynamic into our lives. Three months into the process, I was running ragged. I was trying my best to finish out commitments I'd made before the girls came to live with us, and was increasingly frustrated with what felt like the utter chaos my life had become. I tried my best to focus on the girls' immediate needs while still keeping my boys' lives as steady as I could because that was all I could really control.

Faith was making so much progress. Her vocabulary was improving. Her general health was better. She was becoming more comfortable with us and building appropriate boundaries with strangers. Emma was growing and moving around more. Three months after Emma came to us, the doctor took her off her high calorie formula because she had skyrocketed up the chart to the 95th percentile for height and weight. Every day, we celebrated some kind of developmental milestone.

During one particularly challenging weekend when all four of my kids were sick, and I hadn't had any sleep, I got a text from my friend that said, "Check your porch!" I found a dozen donuts and a 20 oz.

coffee. These gestures helped me see that the good always outweighed the bad.

At the same time, our life was ruled by someone else's calendar. Despite the fact that the biological parents were unreliable, no one made any effort to change the schedule, so we had to be ready for visits no matter what. I kept detailed notes, so I knew that their mom had shown up to roughly one-third of her visits. Of those visits, she ended almost all of them early. Emma's dad's numbers were slightly higher but not stellar. In order to have the girls ready for these visits (that were not actually happening most of the time), I had to put them to bed at 6:30, so they could get down for morning naps before they left for a visit at noon.

Facebook: February 17, 2017
The girls had a visitation scheduled for today, and the boys had early release, so I told them we could take advantage of some mom + big kid time by seeing at $2 movie.
It's 72° and sunny out, so Will asked if we could roll down the windows on the way. After a few minutes, he said, "This day makes me have feelings. Like I want to cry tears of joy."
And then he asked if I would play, "Free Bird."
#thisiseleven #mineallmine #TGIF

August Leia (the version of me who always signs up for things I regret later in the school year) had volunteered to run the second grade Valentine's Day party, which conveniently was happening right in the middle of a visit. I looked forward to being able to focus fully on Ben and his friends. An hour before I needed to be at the school armed with snacks and activities, I got a text from the case assistant that the visit was canceled. I had woken up two babies from naps and was in the middle of diapering and dressing them because she was supposed to be at my house within minutes. There was no way I could run a class party with two babies on my hips. Enter my mom, Super Mimi, to save the day. Things like this happened more often than not, and Mimi couldn't always cover for me. I'd often have to drag two babies to a doctor's appointment with me or cancel my plans altogether. The only thing that was consistent was the inconsistency.

Facebook: March 3, 2017
I'll be writing a real update soon about where we are with our girls, but I feel like it has been too long, so here's a tiny snippet.
Both girls are growing and learning and excelling at life.
Just this week, F figured out ow to blow a recorder (as opposed to humming), and E has perfected her aim so that she only spits up on her feet—never herself. They're basically geniuses.
#worstinstrumentever #barfyshoes #fostercare #babygirls #andthentherewerefour #TGIF

We had planned a ski trip to Utah before we had the girls. Some long-time friends had the idea to meet in Park City, Utah as a reunion of sorts. Because the girls were both under two, it was just a matter of adding them to our tickets as lap children, and we could be on our way. I was slightly concerned about getting travel consents from the case manager, but a couple of weeks before we were leaving, both Jessica and Chad dropped completely out of the picture. It was the first time that we had a quiet break in the storm.

The case manager had put a plan in place stating that they were to confirm via text or phone call within 24 hours of each visit in an effort to provide a little more stability for me. If some kind of communication didn't happen, the case manager reserved the right to cancel the visit. This gave us a little more breathing room, as we knew a day in advance that our schedule was changing instead of mere hours or even minutes.

For a host of reasons I wouldn't know until later, both parents stopped confirming their visits and then stopped communicating altogether.

During this time period, I applied for travel consent, and without any problems, it was granted. We were going on vacation, and the girls could come with us. It couldn't have come at a better time. I needed some downtime. I needed to get away from the madness. I needed to think about something other than the infuriating nonsense that was our "schedule."

The night we were trying to figure out how to get six people, four suitcases, a snowboard, a pack and play, a stroller, and two car seats onto a plane, I questioned our sanity, but then Scott and I had this conversation that might be the most accurate depiction of our entire life together.

Me: I'll figure it out.

Scott: Remember we all love each other, and this is going to be fun.

Me: As long as you do what I tell you, everything will be fine.

Scott: Always.

In those first few months of fostering, I was doing the heavy lifting, and Scott stood by ready for instructions. We made a good team because I was built for advocating for the underdog, and he was built for taming my emails down, so I didn't come across as belligerent. But as my stress levels went up, I felt more and more disconnected from him and alone in the fight. His normal, everyday activities weren't affected negatively by the addition of these two babies. He was a great dad to them and partner to me at the end of the day when I needed someone else to do bathtime while I breathed, but he wasn't fighting the systemic nonsense that I was from dawn to dusk, and I didn't do a great job of including him in those fights.

In addition to the work I was doing on behalf of the girls, I felt the stress of making sure Scott's life and the boys' lives remained undisturbed. Typing this out in black and white is painful because I recognize the absurdity. I thought I was going to be able to successfully carry the burden for all of us. Carrying that weight alone wasn't sustainable, and I distinctly remember one conversation about how I didn't feel like Scott and I were on the same page. I was screaming at the top of my lungs, and Scott sat still. He listened to me rage, and I don't think he blinked once. At one point, he started to say something, and I cut him off shouting, "NOBODY CARES ABOUT WHAT IS HAPPENING TO THESE BABIES EXCEPT ME, AND I NEED YOU TO BE AS ANGRY AS I AM."

He responded by saying he heard me, and that's really all I needed at that moment. I needed someone to acknowledge my anger and not tell me what to do with it. Saying it out loud also made me realize that the fire was engulfing me because I wasn't letting anyone else help me put it out. Instead, I was running into hay bale after hay bale, adding fuel to the fire and setting other things ablaze as I went.

Learning to communicate with Scott better and with other trusted advisors was a crucial part of staying afloat. I have since learned how to better manage my secondary trauma through Laura van Dernoot Lipsky's book, *Trauma Stewardship*. She speaks directly to any work that involves taking care of people, animals, and our planet. She writes:

We understand that this is an incredible honor as well as a tremendous responsibility. We know that as stewards, we create a space for and honor others' hardship and suffering, and yet we do not assume their pain as our own ... We develop and maintain a long-term strategy that enables us to remain whole and helpful to others and our surroundings even amid great challenges. To participate in trauma stewardship is to always remember the privilege and sacredness of being called to help.

Later she adds:

Trauma stewardship calls us to engage oppression and trauma ... by caring for, tending to, and responsibly guiding other beings who are struggling. At the same time, we do not internalize others' struggles or assume them as our own ... we must respond to even the most urgent human and environmental conditions in a sustainable and intentional way. By developing the deep sense of awareness needed to care for ourselves while caring for others and the world around us, we can greatly enhance our potential to work for change, ethically and with integrity, for generations to come.

In addition to being grateful for how Scott and others handled me with patience, I was grateful to my friends in social justice circles who reminded me that being the savior of the world was not my job nor in my skill set. Much of the inner work I still needed to do was in respecting the process—the parts that angered me and didn't go as quickly as I wanted them to go—and the people who didn't do things the way I thought best. This is the hard, humbling work that no one wants to talk about. Yes, the system needs an overhaul, but nothing would ever change if I didn't start by healing the parts of me that contributed to the problem.

Part of the healing I needed would come in the form of taking a much needed break. One such break was meeting my friends Sarah and Maro and their families in Park City, Utah. We were flying in from southern Illinois. Sarah's family drove down from Portland, Oregon. Maro's family flew in from Jacksonville, Florida. Despite the fact that we lived about as far away from each other as we could within the continental United States, these women were intimately invested in our case. Sarah and her husband, Kris, had walked through an adoption with some of their closest friends in recent years. Maro, and her husband, Rich, had just adopted their daughter from foster care earlier that year. Among us, we had nine children, and the days we spent in Utah were filled with big meals and loud voices and all the marks of friendship done right.

During our trip, I felt a sense of peace as I watched Scott pull the girls around on a sled in their snowsuits. It was the first time that I said things out loud like "our four kids" and "our oldest daughter." Even with a millisecond of a pause before saying those words, I gave myself permission to say them. When we were traveling home, Faith dragged one of our rolling bags around the airport. An older woman, enchanted by her cherubic face leaned down and said to her, "Aren't you a doll? You look just like your mommy." That was me. I was her mommy. I didn't correct her.

I was still hyper aware that nearly four months into this case, we were nowhere near adoption, but my heart was softening to the idea while my head reminded me that the end goal was still reunification. I wrestled with thoughts when I should have been sleeping. *I love them so much even though they aren't mine. We have to help Jessica get them back. She is doing nothing to get them back—how long until the court decides she is unfit? Has she had enough time to prove she can be a good parent to them? She is their mother—that will never change. Her trauma is too great to overcome—even if she was doing the work to heal, which she's not, she will need years of help to be able to give them a good life. I cannot imagine our family without these two little girls. How am I going to help the boys process the loss when they're gone? What is a reasonable amount of time to give parents the opportunity to get their kids back? How many chances do they deserve? Do they deserve any chances when they continue to make poor choices? How do I protect these kids from an apathetic system? How can I show Jessica how to be a good parent? Is this a lost cause?*

CHAPTER SIX
The Boys

Scott and I got married a hot second after we graduated from college. In a traditional wedding at the Presbyterian church where Scott had been baptized as a baby, we stood in front of God and a few hundred friends to pledge our love. Scott would start pilot training a few weeks later after we had a honeymoon and our first holiday season as a married couple. I was finishing my first semester of grad school. We were young, but the timing was right.

Almost a year into our marriage, I was working a temp job at a chemical plant on the outskirts of the sleepy town of Enid, Oklahoma and finishing my masters degree. At his pilot training graduation, the night we found out we'd be moving to Charleston, SC, we told our families who had gathered for the big event that we were going to have a baby.

For me, getting married seemed a logical next step at that juncture of our life. Having a baby was my idea first, and with what I now see as a giant stroke of luck, we conceived easily. When I told Scott I wanted to have a baby, his response was something like, "What? Oh, okay." I think he was surprised because he didn't picture adding to our family so soon. The vast majority of our friends were still single, many of them with no prospects or even the desire to be married. Having a baby would make us the weird old people in our friend group.

I had wanted to be a mom for as long as my memories existed. As a little girl, I played house sometimes, marrying my friends, but most of my preschool imaginative play centered on giving birth and raising oodles of babies. Probably as a result of spending a lot of one-on-one time with my mom, my greatest ambition was to be a mother. At 24, I was months away from checking off the grad school box. I was trying to decide what having a career as a military spouse was going to look like. I wasn't sure what the future held, but I walked into the decision to become a mother with complete confidence that I was made to be one.

A couple years later, one of my friends who was struggling with postpartum depression asked me, "Do you really love being a mom as much as you say you do?" I have answered that question over and over with a resounding yes. In fact, I've been known to say that being a mom is the thing I am best at. I took piano lessons a few years ago, and after a year of working with a teacher, I was about as good as my third grader. I had a friend growing up who could sit down at a keyboard and play entire songs by ear. It was an effortless, natural talent. Did he hit the wrong keys sometimes? Sure. Did he have to practice before big performances? Of course. But there was something inside of him that couldn't be taught. And that's what it feels like to be a mom for me.

Having Will opened facets of my heart I didn't know existed. With Scott on the road most of the time, Will and I were best buddies. We binged reality TV and explored the Lowcountry together. Aside from not sleeping at night, he was an easy baby. Often, I would catch the side eye from other people in restaurants or museums. I could see the looks on their faces: *what is that lady doing bringing a baby in here?* Before long, those same strangers would be complimenting him on being such a great kid and offering to hold him while I gathered our things to leave.

I was content to have an only child. He was the perfect little side-kick, everything I had hoped for when I told Scott I was ready to have a baby. The second time around, Scott was the one who felt strongly about having another one. He grew up with a sister and felt like Will could benefit from having a sibling. As an only child myself, I wasn't completely convinced that we needed another child, but Scott was sure it was the right move.

Ben's labor was fast and uncomplicated, and seconds after he was born, I had this thought that I kept a secret for a long time: *I could have ten more kids*. I can't explain that. This defies logic, but there was something about seeing Will and Ben together that made me understand why people have big families. When Ben was breastfeeding for the first time, Will asked if he was having breakfast and then offered him some Skittles. The next day, supervised by visiting grandparents, Will showed up at the hospital to visit his new brother dressed as Batman.

The hardest moment for me in motherhood thus far was easily the transition from having one baby to having two. I had enrolled Will in a parents' morning out program two days a week at a local church because I thought having a few hours alone with Ben would be nice, and Will would enjoy the interaction with teachers and friends. At almost three and a half, he was still not convinced that anywhere was as fun as right next to his mama. He struggled at drop off for longer than I would have liked, and even though his teachers said he recovered and had good days at school, the separation was still rough on my postpartum psyche to look at his weepy, cartoonishly large blue eyes every time he said, "Please come back. I will miss you so much."

Aside from these emotional goodbyes, getting him to "school" on time meant waking up a sleeping baby to nurse earlier than he would have on his natural rhythm. The drive meant loading said baby into his car seat which he hated with the heat of one million suns. Ben screamed the entire ride and only stopped when I took him out and calmed him down by nursing him again in the parking lot from the front seat of my car. We made the same shrieking drive home, and though I understand how time works, it felt like every day our one-on-one time was over before it began as I had to start the whole process over again to pick Will up two and a half hours later.

I called my mom one morning while Ben nursed in the car. I cried as I told her that I felt like an absolute loon these two days that Will went to school. After listening to me cry for a few minutes, she said, "You know you're in charge, and you don't have to take him to school, right?" I had forgotten. I really had. In the haze of middle of the night feedings and toddler entertaining, I had forgotten I was in charge. I spent the rest of the day weighing the pros and cons of stopping the madness. In the end, I kept Will in school, and eventually Ben hated his car seat a little less, and those mornings did turn into quality one-on-one time.

Like most of my freak out moments (of which I've had many), the solution was less tangible and more about realigning my mindset. I could have taken Will out of his two day program for a month to give us all a breather, and that probably would have helped, too, but the main thing I needed was to remember who I was. I think the reason our transition to four wasn't as difficult as people anticipated was because I had eleven years of parenting under my belt that taught me to stay flexible and remember who was in charge.

Parenting kids under five has a way of pushing us to our limits. We are tired. We are trying to do too many things at once. Every day, sometimes more than once a day, we find ourselves navigating a new transition. Just when we think we've got the nap schedule down, the baby drops a nap. The toddler spins out of control because we've given him the wrong cup at lunchtime. Life is unpredictable, and I can't think of many other situations where our expectations so vividly do not match our reality.

Remember you're in charge. That's a mantra that still comes to mind often. As a military spouse and foster mom, I am presented with situations all the time that are completely out of my control. Our "normal" was thinking Dad was going to be home at a certain time or on a certain day, and then he wasn't—because a jet broke or because he pulled down an unexpected trip or some other valid clandestine reason. Scott has been on the receiving end of countless diatribes from me about how someone in the Air Force needs to get their poop in a pile, so I can plan my life. (I am a delight to be married to sometimes.) We've rescheduled vacations and birthday parties. We've had Thanksgiving dinner with Scott's disembodied head on the computer screen at the end of the table. We make it work in whatever way we can because we don't have a choice so much of the time. As a military spouse, I've had to learn that I am in charge of what I'm in charge of, and I have to let the rest go.

Stepping into the tumultuous, nonsensical, unpredictable world of foster care felt like home. In the same way that I have always known I would be a great mom, I knew I could handle being a foster parent. Parenting two babies so close in age was not without challenge, but I was older and arguably wiser, and I had two of the best helpers in Will and Ben to help me keep the boat afloat.

The main reason we waited to become a foster family as long as we did is because the first nine years of our marriage were ruled by deployments and other military-related unpredictability. The second reason we waited is because we wanted our boys to have shared agency in the decision. When I was pregnant with Ben, Will told everyone about his sister, "Syball." When we found out we were having another boy, we successfully transferred this idea to a stuffed friend from Build-a-Bear, and Will got used to the idea of having a brother instead.

After Ben was born, Will frequently asked for a sister. Every time he asked, I told him I was done having kids, knowing full well that the possibility of adoption would remain on the table. I distinctly remember having a conversation about what adoption was when he went through a phase where he was obsessed with the movie version of *Stuart Little*, and I had to explain to him that if we ever adopted, we would not be adopting a talking mouse. His dreams were momentarily crushed.

In trying to decide if the timing was right for our family to foster, Scott and I talked at length with the boys. We knew that fostering was a family experience, so the boys gave a lot of input before we got a placement. Later in our case, when we made the decision to limit the number of full-time kids in our home to four total (including our biological children), it was in large part because Will, our oldest, said he felt like four was the right number.

We also walked into fostering with open eyes and hearts. In our conversations as a family, we focused on fostering, not adopting. I didn't have any reservations about how everyone would handle an adoption, but I did have concerns about what might happen if we fostered children repeatedly and then saw them go back to their families of origin. We did our best to prepare the boys for that eventuality, stressing that our first priority was to support kids who needed a safe place until they could reunite. We likened it to having cousins come visit—we would love our kids in care, have fun with them, treat them like family, knowing they had homes somewhere else. We talked about how the kids who came to live with us might not have great behavior, so our job was to teach them how to be kind. We talked about how the kids who came to live with us might have health issues, so our job was to be gentle with them on hard days. We talked about how we might welcome big kids or babies, one at a time or siblings. We talked about how they might stay with us for two weeks or a year.

Scott is an Eagle Scout, and both boys were working toward the same. Everyone knew the importance of being prepared, and we did our best to set up our whole family for success. But big choices like this—joining the military, getting married, having a baby, fostering—always come with a dose of the great unknown. And that's okay.

Facebook: May 25, 2017

This week has been … not good on the foster care front. Believe me when I tell you that I would love to share every infuriating detail with you. Alas, I cannot. I can tell you that it's nothing so terrible that the girls are being moved or anything like that, but some decisions have been made that are not in their best interest, and I have spent a lot of time sending strongly worded emails to people who should do better. Strongly worded emails are exhausting, you guys. I would love it if you would share some things that are happening in your lives that will help restore my faith in humanity. I will accept funny memes, personal stories, inspiring articles—anything that will help me hate people less. Thanks in advance!

CHAPTER SEVEN
The Struggle

At the beginning of each foster care case, service plans are put into place for every parent involved, and a "permanency goal" is set. At the time of this writing, Illinois ranks 51st in the nation (behind all other states and Puerto Rico) for the length of time it takes to settle cases, whether the result is reunification or adoption. For our case, the original permanency goal was to return the children home within five months. As foster parents, we were not privy to exact information about the girls' parents' service plans, but typically, parents who are working toward a return home goal will have to complete services such as parenting classes, anger management classes, drug counseling, mental health counseling, and various assessments. These service plans are tailored to each parent according to why children are brought into care.

Because none of the parents in our case were making significant progress on their service plans, the case manager anticipated a change in the permanency goal at the next hearing. Counterintuitively, instead of moving toward terminating parental rights due to lack of progress, we anticipated that the timeline would be extended to give the girls' parents more time to complete their service plans. We were told that more than likely the timeline would be changed from five months to one year, meaning Faith and Emma would be in our care at least until the end of 2017.

Permanency hearings are set for every six months automatically, so we would go to court in July to hear about the progress of our case, and in mid-May our case manager asked us to sign concurrent planning paperwork as part of this process. While we would still be working toward reunification, this paperwork stated that if the girls' parents were unable to complete their service plans, we would be willing to adopt them. This statement is an important part of foster care because many cases linger for years on end because there isn't a back up plan. Parents are given years to work service plans and children are held in limbo, often bouncing from foster home to foster home, because no one is willing to adopt them.

When we decided to be foster parents, it was not with adoption in mind, but as with much of the way this case played out, when we were asked the question of whether or not we were willing to adopt given the chance, it was an easy yes. Emma had lived with us for six of the nine months of her life at this point. Faith had only been with us for three months, but in that short time, she'd made strong attachments with our family and friends. If their biological parents were unable to care for them long-term, there was no reason their fate should be in question.

Around the same time we signed paperwork stating that our family was a solid Plan B, I got a text from our case manager. It was a Monday, and I was exhausted and already on edge. Jessica had all but disappeared for several weeks, resurfacing for a few visits with the girls, during which the level of care was unacceptable. The girls were coming home filthy from crawling around a dirty apartment floor. Their diapers were not changed during visits that lasted several hours. At one point, in a why-do-I-have-to-say-this-out-loud moment, I had a conversation with the case assistant during which I asked her if she could please politely ask that the girls not be given Mountain Dew. I was happy to send along baby food, formula, and snacks if it meant keeping them from eating chocolate pudding and Fruit Loops for dinner. Technically, biological parents are required to provide diapers and food during visits, but I was past adhering to the rules for the rules' sake. I wanted the kids to be safe and clean and to not fall apart from sugar crashes and digestional disasters.

So when I got the text from our case manager that Faith would now start visits with her dad on Saturday mornings, I lost it. I was not kind. I did not measure my words. I unleashed a text rant that was met by relative silence from the case manager. In hindsight, she did exactly what she should have done because I was unable to have a reasonable conversation at that moment. It was a Monday morning like most. I was catching up on laundry, playing with babies, and attempting to answer emails from my phone. The text stopped me in my tracks. I sat on the floor and pulled both girls into my lap and cried. In five days, I'd put Faith in a car to visit a virtual stranger.

The root of my frustration was in the fact that five months into this case, Faith's dad had never attempted to complete his service plan. He had not even shown up for his DNA test when ordered a month into the case. I did not understand why a child would be required to go to visits with a person who was not confirmed to be her parent. Because he was listed as her father on the birth certificate, he was considered her "putative father" and allowed visits. Within a couple of months, he was proven to be her biological father when he finally submitted to a DNA test, but at the time all I could think was how unjust this felt that he could be a ghost for five months, make one phone call, and be granted weekly visits. I demanded to know why he wasn't at least required to submit to a DNA test before visits started and was given no answers—no one owed me an explanation, and it felt like my opinion on the matter was not valued.

Our saving grace and the only reason I was able to cope with the stress of knowing these babies did not seem to be anyone's priority in the decision-making process was that all of these visits were supervised by a case assistant. The case assistant's job was to take notes during the visits and report back to the case manager about any concerns. If a child's safety was at risk or visitation rules were not being followed, the case assistant had the right to end visits. For the entirety of our case, the case assistants carried the burden of our expectations—that the children be protected and that the parents be treated fairly. Knowing the case assistants were there to act as intermediaries calmed my anxiety around the things we were regularly witnessing.

Writing about this aspect of our case without sounding judgmental of the people involved is hard. There were many times throughout our case that I was frustrated with the case managers or the case assistants who made decisions under the banner of "policy and procedure." There were many times when I was disappointed and angry about things the girls' parents did or didn't do. There were many times I overstepped my bounds as a foster parent and blurred the line between professional advocacy for vulnerable children and my personal passion for protecting people I loved.

Here's the thing about this—why foster care is so hard. People are so dang people-y sometimes. Everyone involved is under a tremendous amount of stress and very few of the people involved are doing the work they need to do to take care of themselves first. Emotions are raw. Tempers are short. Everyone has the tendency to operate from defensive positions for a variety of reasons. Case managers have been burned. Biological parents are experiencing the worst moment of their lives—losing their children in the middle of dealing with immense personal crises. Foster parents are trying their best to serve the children at the request of the state while not taking the broken system personally despite having virtually no rights or decision-making agency. And the children in the middle of all this? I continue to be righteously indignant thinking about how children in care are held in limbo, further traumatizing them in the process.

More than ever before in my life, every day brought me another opportunity to lay bare my humanity—having to admit that someone else's ideas might be better than mine, apologizing for being disrespectful, learning to make peace with and funnel my anger in productive ways. Every day also brought me another opportunity to forgive other people's greatest faults. What a tremendous and infuriating challenge to be asked to build bridges of grace and forgiveness over and over and over again.

Faith began visiting her first dad every Saturday for two hours. He took her to McDonald's and bought her ice cream. She was able to see her two biological brothers who lived with him. I tried to focus on the good when I learned that the reason they went to McDonald's every week was because his home had been ruled unsafe. I also learned that one of the reasons he had to meet in a public space was because Jessica had moved back in with him, and while she was home, she was not allowed to be at "his" visits. Unlike my relationship with Jessica, I had a hard time humanizing Don because I'd never met him. The information about him available to me was not helpful either.

When his visits started, Jessica was 21, and he was 53. They had three children together, the oldest of whom was six and all of whom had been conceived before Jessica's eighteenth birthday. Jessica had shared openly the details about how their "relationship" began, and I made myself physically sick thinking about it in regard to Faith spending time with him. So much of their story is not mine to tell, so I will only speak for how this affected me.

When my mom was pregnant with me, my parents fostered one of our family members for a short time while her parents were in jail. When her mom was released, the court decided to return her home. For her entire childhood, she suffered the consequences of that choice, experiencing abuse and neglect at the hands of people who should have protected her. As an adult, she went on to have kids removed from her care as she struggled to find a way to live. Her story is one of the reasons I felt drawn to foster care. Today, I don't see her in person often because we live in different states, but I follow her life on social media where she often talks about protecting kids from predators. Sometimes she posts pictures of beautiful, detailed drawings remarking that she has always loved art. Recently, we had a conversation about a book we both read and loved. She is living her life and raising some of her children in the best way she knows how, but I think about how her life would have been different if she had remained with my parents. My drive to protect children from abuse is deeply personal.

With some regularity, I see stories on social media, mugshots of men and women who have been arrested for raping children. The comment sections are full of vitriol. Some might call it righteous anger. The way that our court system dehumanizes victims of rape and assault is appalling, and I have lost sleep over stories about strangers who have not seen justice for the ways they have been victimized. For my own sanity, I've had to stop reading those stories. I don't mean I'm turning a blind eye to the atrocities committed by deeply troubled and in some cases evil people. Instead, I look for ways to affect change. Feeling sick and angry does not help victims. As a society, we have to push for better legislation and shed light on judges who slap perpetrators on the wrist and send them out into the world to offend again.

It is through this lens that I viewed Faith's interaction with her biological father. It is through this lens that I found myself in meetings with agency officials asking over and over how he could be a viable option with a return home goal. I was met with defensive responses about how I needed to be careful about the terminology I was using, how I had to allow the process to work, and how they had to provide a service plan because he asked for one. Even though he had an active criminal case for his interaction with Jessica when she was a minor, I was told none of that had anything to do with family court. At one point, there was a conversation about the fact that if Faith was returned to him, Emma might go with her in order to keep the siblings together—an unlikely scenario, but a conversation that led to off-the-charts anxiety for me.

46

All of this stiffened my resolve and made me more protective of the girls. As Jessica continued to flail and Chad disappeared, the idea that the court would consider separating the girls and returning Faith to this man was gut-wrenching and ludicrous. I became fixated in an unhealthy way. When our case worker told us she was changing positions within the agency, and we would be getting a new worker, I spiraled. I couldn't eat, or I ate too much at 2:00 in the morning. I stayed up all night reading Illinois foster care laws, making notes for my lawyer friends to interpret parts I didn't understand. I typed up ranty letters to The System. Who was I going to send these to? I don't know. I found myself in tears multiple times a day, and my anxiety presented as rapid heart palpitations.

It felt like the life we were building for these girls was falling apart and despite my every effort, there was nothing I could do to change it.

CHAPTER EIGHT
The Short-Termer

Before we decided to join the fostering community, we had several friends who inspired us to do so. When I was right out of college, my friend, Sarah, provided respite care for about ten kids while she was still in grad school. Respite care exists for short term support of foster parents. Sometimes foster parents have to travel and cannot take their kids with them. Sometimes they just need a break. Sarah was an art teacher at a high potential school in Oklahoma City where my mom worked, and I admired her heart for the way she threw herself into loving every kid who came into her classroom. She felt compelled to become a respite caregiver when she saw some of her students bouncing around foster homes and group homes, and she knew coming to stay with her would be a much better solution for these kids who needed a temporary home. After Sarah married her husband, Lee, they hosted about fifteen more respite kids before eventually committing to being full-time foster parents.

Sarah's experience with respite care was the first close up view I had of fostering. When Scott and I first started talking about how we fit in the world of foster care, we thought this might be a way to dip our toes in the water while meeting a need. During training, we decided we were all in, but we also let our agency know we were willing to provide respite care as needed.

On Mother's Day weekend after the girls came to live with us and in the middle of sorting out the new changes to Faith's schedule, we were asked to provide respite care for a six-year-old boy who was living with his aunt and uncle. His biological parents were struggling with addiction, and his aunt and uncle had taken him in after being told it would be a short-term placement. Nine months into the process, his behavior was becoming increasingly difficult for them to handle. As they anticipated a likely parental termination, things came to a head.

When his case manager called us, she said his aunt and uncle needed a break after a particularly bad episode. We were around for the weekend with no real plans, so C came to stay with us. She dropped him off at our house on a Friday afternoon with a bag of well-packed clothes and no instructions. His case manager said she would pick him back up for school Monday morning.

C was quiet and polite. He had a close buzz cut and freckles across his nose. When I asked him if he wanted something to eat or drink, he asked if we had any icy water. When the boys came home from school, the three of them raced outside to jump on the trampoline in the backyard. If I had had no context, I would have looked out the window and thought the boys were playing with a friend from the neighborhood.

The weather was that perfect summer-is-coming warm with a coolness in the air from spring still hanging on. We had pizza night like we did every Friday. We spent Saturday lounging around the house playing board games and Pokémon. That evening, we set up the projector and movie screen on the porch outside, and all five kids piled onto blankets and pillows to watch *Sing*, a movie that satisfied the preteens and toddlers alike.

Scott and I sat together watching the kids interact and joked that after three it all feels the same. I wondered if this would create a crack in the "four is enough" mindset. Because his job takes him away so often, I found myself feeling like I was on an island most days. I recognized seeds of resentment taking place in my heart. Even though we were "in this together," I felt like his emotional investment was a fraction of mine.

What I realized that weekend in particular was that Scott was far more invested than I was giving him credit for, and most of my negative thought patterns came from the fact that I spent so much time thinking instead of talking. When we were actually hand-in-hand, face-to-face, heart-to-heart—we were a great team. Frankly, Scott's heart is much softer than mine, and I realized that the disconnect I was feeling had so much more to do with the fact that I wasn't letting him in. He was essentially an overlooked star player sitting on the bench whispering, "Put me in, coach." I resolved to communicate better and to trust him with more of the workload, including carrying some of the emotional burden that was crippling me.

On Sunday morning, Scott ran out to get donuts. C wanted a chocolate long john. We sat around the table together munching on our sweets and laughing at little boy jokes. When I put him to bed that evening, I felt like he was mine even though I knew he'd be gone in the morning.

As the rest of us buzzed around Monday morning getting ready for the school day, C sat on the floor looking out the window of our French doors that led to the side porch of our house. He wrapped his scrawny first grader arms around his knees, and his bag full of freshly washed clothes sat beside him. He was wearing a navy blue Superman shirt with a cape attached at the back. I hoped he would return to his aunt and uncle's house feeling loved, and I hoped this weekend respite was the break they needed to keep soldiering on through a difficult situation.

I'd taken several pictures of him throughout the weekend to send to the case manager, so she could share with his family. As he walked to the car, I took one last picture of this six-year-old boy and a woman whose long day was beginning with a 45 minute drive to drop him off at school. He glanced over his shoulder as I took the picture, and the look in his eyes was a mixture of happiness and fear. That is not a combination of emotions that any child should ever feel.

Facebook: June 14, 2017
I sat 9mo E down in her high chair next to Will when I was getting dinner on the table. I walked out of the room and heard a loud thump and then a cry from the baby. I asked what happened, and Will shouted back to me, "E knocked my book off the table."
As she continued to cry, I heard him say to her, "It's okay, sister. Don't cry. I'm not mad at you. People are more important than things." So, an otherwise crappy day was redeemed because that's how this works.
#theylisten #theyrepeat #kidwisdom #thekidsareallright

In quiet moments, I pull that picture up and think about him because C moved on with his life, and things did not go well. When he returned home, he lashed out at his aunt and uncle and said some things that scared them. They were tired and trying to raise two younger biological children. They had the added weight of family drama that kinship placements always have. When they decided to foster C, they hoped his parents would be able to get their lives together, so he could return home. That wasn't happening.

In our experience, we know what it's like to try to balance a relationship with biological parents, but it is much easier to create boundaries when the people are not related to us. Fostering a family member's child comes with so much risk—families are torn apart sometimes. How do you navigate holiday gatherings when all a kid wants is to see his mom, but she's not allowed to be there? How do you love your sister when she hates you for "taking" her child? C's aunt and uncle were already fatigued, and the break they got was affirmation that they no longer wanted him in their home.

Of course, that caused me grief for C, but I also sympathized with their tough decision.

A couple of days after C left, we got a call asking if we would take him full-time. Scott was leaving for a five-day trip, and my parents were traveling that week as well. Saying yes would mean having five kids by myself, one of which would have to be driven to school in a different county every day. I felt the weight of that responsibility—caring for a newborn, a toddler who was just three months into the process of learning how to be a part of our family, and managing both the physical and emotional logistics of loving my two original kids. Scott and Will both said that four kids was our limit, and while I didn't feel the same, I had to trust their instincts on this.

Bringing C into our home at that particular juncture felt like the wrong decision. I'm not going to say the decision was unanimous. I would have said yes, but I was not the only person to consider. I didn't call Scott or talk to the boys about the possibility because we'd already had enough conversations about not taking any more permanent placements that I knew what they would say. I waited several hours before calling his case manager back with my answer because it was not a clear cut, peaceful decision. When I called her back, she was disappointed. I could hear the distress in her voice. When I asked what the alternative was, she was vague in responding because the details of his case really weren't my business, but I gathered she was trying to work out a plan that involved grandparents who lived out of state.

The most devastating part came the next day. The case manager called and said C was going to be in-patient at an adolescent psych ward for ten days because of some of his behavior and threatening statements. His aunt and uncle did not want him in their home, and he had nowhere else to go at the moment.

Ten days.

He was six years old.

He had been in my home for three sleeps, and nothing about this kid said "psych ward." Trauma? Yes. Grief? Yes. Anger management issues? I could believe that even though he had not acted out in any way during our time with him. But ten days in the psych ward? That was absurd. But it was also how long the state would pay.

And this is how stories about kids in care who bounce around the system for years without being adopted start. I tried to tell myself that I had to trust my capacity and the capacity of the other people in my home. I tried to tell myself that I could not fix every problem. I tried to tell myself to stay in the moment and take his story one day at a time instead of fixating on projected possibilities. But no amount of mental gymnastics dulled the pain.

Over the next few days, I would learn more details about the case—how he had threatened to burn down the house and hurt his cousins, how during intake he was given an anti-depressant medication before ever seeing a doctor, how he lashed out at all his visitors including his biological mother. The final blow was when I found out that his grand-parents were hesitant but willing to take him short-term, but they were clear about not being able to adopt him.

I enlisted the help of the director of a local nonprofit that provides support to foster families. C needed a permanent home, and I knew they might be able to tap into resources that I didn't have as a new foster parent. I knew C's case manager was trying to solve this problem while juggling dozens of other kids on her caseload. I could not control the chaos, so I had to make peace with trusting the experts to find a solution. Eventually, I got sporadic texts from the case manager letting me know that they believed they had a home for him. Over time, I got fewer texts, and I wasn't sure what happened to C.

I don't know that I will ever get over this. And I don't want to get over it. C is one kid out of thousands who get stuck in limbo in the system. Many of them "age out," and the statistics about jail time, teen pregnancy (ending in generational foster care), high school dropout rates, homelessness, drug and alcohol abuse, and mental illness are devastating. I know of many organizations and individuals who are working hard to put their fingers in the proverbial dam, but we have to start thinking in terms of how we stop the flood in the first place.

About a year after all of this happened, I texted his case manager asking how he was doing. She texted me back that after some time, he had gone to live with his grandparents out of state, and he was doing "miraculously well."

For every happy-ish ending like C's, there are dozens of stories about kids being moved over and over and over again, their behavioral issues and diagnoses worsening with each placement. These kids who never find their forever families end up in group homes or bad foster homes where their needs are still not met. Then they age out.

In contrast, my day-to-day job was to observe what happens when children are provided safety and security. The girls were growing and forming attachments and developing quickly into happy, healthy humans. Even with ongoing and mind-numbing frustrations with navigating the system, I knew that foster care had the potential to help children heal. I was watching healing happen every day in my home.

When I lie awake at night under the weight of everything foster care brings, stories like C's haunt me most.

We have to find a better way.

CHAPTER NINE
The Hearing

Five months into our case, I wrote a blog post detailing how our case was officially "concurrently planned" meaning that if the girls did not return home, we would be willing to adopt them. If ever there is a paradigm that's difficult to accept, it's that our daily interactions supported a reunification plan we didn't believe would be successful while wholeheartedly committing to loving these girls forever.

Here is part of what I wrote:

"Until about six weeks ago, I would have characterized the girls' parental involvement as limping toward success, and then everything started heading downhill. We continue to have an immense amount of empathy for the girls' mom, as she is first a young girl who is a product of her environment. It's easy to judge her for the choices she's making if we don't take into account the fact that no one has ever shown her what real love looks like. No one has protected her. No one has taught her right from wrong. In fact, all the people in her life who should have taught her how to be human have actively worked against her for her entire life.

It's heartbreaking and infuriating …

People often say things to me along the lines of "I don't know how you do it" and "That's so hard—I could never do it." Yeah, it is, but not in the ways you think. I've heard sermons in which people have compared our lives to beautiful tapestries. The thing about weaving tapestries is that a weaver creates from the back, so the image she sees for a long time looks like a jumbled mess. I almost pride myself on being someone who can see the beauty in the ordinary most of the time, but this journey feels much messier than anything else I've tried to create with my life.

The other night when I should have been sleeping, I watched a YouTube video about weaving tapestries because I couldn't get this notion out of my head, and I learned something pretty stunning.

Tapestries are woven horizontally across a loom of taut vertical lines. In a massive undertaking called "warping," the loom is created by looping yarn over and over again. Once the bundle is large enough, the weaver starts warping another long thread. That's what each week feels like right now. We all feel a little warped as we loop around and around and around the same drama, same concerns, same feelings. And then we feel weary when we have to start again.

Each warp loop is then braided and stretched across the metal beams, meticulously and evenly spread. It's a process that requires attention to detail and time, much like the amount of effort and time I spend every day keeping track of paperwork and making phone calls and trying to ensure that we always have our ducks in a row.

Once the warp is on the beams, the next step is to apply tension through stretching. OOF. Yeah.

Only after the warping and stretching can the weaver begin creating her artwork. Here's the part I found most fascinating—as the weaver moves the yarn through the vertical lines, she gazes through to a mirror. The mirror reflects her artwork in reverse. The challenge of fostering is like this—I'm constantly looking in the mirror trying to figure out if I'm doing it right, and I can see what I'm doing, but it often feels backwards.

Nothing about this feels natural.

I am mothering someone else's children. I love someone else's chil-dren. It's a sea of emotions difficult to navigate. If I keep my head down like the weaver, all I can see is a jumble of threads, but if I look at the reflection in the mirror, I see some semblance of beauty even if it isn't the exact version of beauty I'm aiming for."

In Illinois, foster parents are not required to attend court, but we were counseled by many people to go. At permanency hearings, case managers testify to whether parents are making satisfactory or unsat-isfactory progress. If a parent has completed his or her service plan, the judge can rule to start the reunification process. If a parent has not complied with the state's requirements, the judge can adjust the goal.

Our first permanency hearing was scheduled for July of 2017. The girls had been in care for seven months. While we didn't have access to information about what their parents were required to complete, we knew from the inconsistency of visits and the state in which the girls often returned to our home, that Jessica's service plan was probably unsatisfactory. This was confirmed by the case manager on the stand. It was at that time that we learned that Em-ma's dad, Chad, was sleeping through many of his visits. Faith's dad, Don, had only been requesting visits for about six weeks at that time.

Chad did not come to court. Don and Jessica both came to court. We learned that Don's criminal case finished that same week, and he was on probation for two years. He would not serve jail time as he pleaded down from a felony to a misdemeanor, but part of his probation was that he was not allowed to see Jessica, the victim of his crime, outside of interaction involving their children.

Telling this part of the story is difficult because I want more than anything to respect our girls' first parents at all times, but watching them interact was a little surreal. She was an adult now, so their relationship was no longer illegal, but I still had a hard time wrapping my mind around all of this. I also started to understand why he had shown up out of the blue asking for visits. Jessica was not secretive about the fact that she knew she wasn't going to be able to get her children back. She spoke openly with me about how she was trying to convince Don to fight for Faith and Emma to live with him, and then she would be able to see them whenever she wanted. The kind of intelligence required to survive in this world is a skill that she'd been honing for years. I couldn't help but think what her life would be like if she wasn't constantly in survival mode. Jessica was staying in Don's apartment at the time the verdict came down, so everything was a bit of a mess.

If I could describe Don at that hearing in one word, it would be that he was angry. He didn't lash out at us in the hallway before we went in, but for obvious reasons, he wasn't warm. I wasn't sure what to do when I caught his eye. Smile? Look away? My feelings about his involvement with Jessica, my feelings about him showing up late to the game when his daughter was brought into care, my feelings about why we were all in this courtroom—none of that really mattered. He was a complete stranger, and nothing I knew about him made me like him.

But he was Faith's dad.

And I kept reminding myself of that. We loved her fiercely. We wanted her to have a good life. We were providing the best care we could. Based on what we knew about her family of origin and the possibility of where she could return home, we thought the best place for her to thrive was in our home with her sister, but we also knew that our opinion meant very little in that courtroom. We weren't even required to attend. We spelled our names for the court reporter and then sat silently for the remainder of the hearing. Nothing we did would sway the judge's decision in any way because that is not the role of the foster parent. Feeling powerless in a fight for a child's life is one of the worst pains I've known in my lifetime. I have since thought many times of the pain my children will process as they learn the details of their early lives, and I hope I can remain the open arms they need as they ask questions.

During the hearing, Don ranted—and I mean that in a literal sense—about the injustice of having his daughter taken away. In a sense, his anger was justified. He had nothing to do with her being taken into state care. The girls were brought into care because of the actions of the other two parents involved. To this day, I've never had a clear understanding of why Faith wasn't put in his care from day one. I'm sure the answer exists, but no one will give me a straight answer. Was it the case manager's decision? Did Don say he couldn't care for her? Either way, she landed with Don's adult daughter before moving to our home.

I don't know what to believe about the beginning of the case, but what I do know is that Don was ordered to take a paternity test and was given a service plan, and he did not pursue either of those things until over five months into the case. Conjecture at this point doesn't help anyone understand, so I try my best to stick to the facts. The man who walked into that courtroom was loaded for bear. He unleashed his fury and was met with a strong, fair response from the judge. The judge said repeatedly, "Sir, I cannot change the past, but you have been given all the information you need to get your daughter back. If you do what the court has asked of you, she will live with you again." Even though we knew this was the goal, I bristled hearing the judge say it out loud.

We had seen Jessica occasionally at doctor's appointments for the girls or at times when I dropped them off at visits instead of the case assistant picking them up throughout the seven months leading up to this day. I was always taken aback at the way she interacted with me. Up to that point, she never seemed angry. She was always respectful, and our conversations flowed easily. She was curious about our family and inquisitive about the girls. She asked genuine questions about parenting that allowed me to mentor her in tiny ways. Even though I knew the news from the stand wasn't going to paint her in a positive light, I still felt heart pangs at the case manager's announcement that she was failing drug tests and not finishing parts of her service plan. The best way to articulate my feelings about Jessica even in those first few months is that I was immensely disappointed and fiercely protective. After one visit, our case assistant, Michelle, told me that Jessica had been asking questions about us and had jokingly said, "I wish they could adopt me."

When Michelle told me that Jessica had asked if we could adopt her, I felt the first stirrings of desire to be more hands-on in Jessica's life. We had been advised by everyone involved to be cautious in our interactions. I understood this advice, but I also felt something counter to that advice in my spirit. Seeing Jessica at court and listening to her failures delineated from a microphone for everyone to hear confirmed that my instincts were right. With the help of the case manager, we came up with a plan. We set up an email address first, something she could check from her phone where I could send pictures and stories about the girls, and she could check in whenever she needed. Within about a month, we exchanged phone numbers for the ease of texting. Shortly after we exchanged phone numbers, Jessica confirmed something I had expected at court. She was pregnant again.

CHAPTER TEN
The Names

I have one regret about the way we shared our story in real time that I hope to remedy here in this book. I regularly blogged and updated a wide circle of people in the beginning of our case. I was always discreet about details, but I tried to be as honest as possible about how foster care was affecting our family. I needed the catharsis of community, but I was also intentional about sharing details that would engage people. In the end, I wanted our story to mean something bigger than what was happening within the walls of our home. I hoped that our story would inspire people to action.

My one regret was that I waited until a couple of months before the girls were officially adopted to let people know that we intended to legally change their names. This is a source of controversy within the adoption community at large. When I finally shared this information with the outer circles of our community, people had an adverse reaction. I'd been referring to the girls as F and E or Sister and Baby for over two years when I shared this information. Of course, the people who saw the girls all the time knew about our intentions, but the decision felt jolting to people who weren't directly connected to our everyday life. I didn't know how big people's feelings would be about this change.

We didn't come to this decision lightly, and announcing their names the first time we were able to show their faces on social media was jarring for some people. In that moment, partially because I was still working out my own conflicted feelings about the issue, I felt defensive and as if I didn't owe anyone an explanation. After all, the people who resisted the idea weren't from our inner circle. Some of them were people I'd never met in real life. However, some of these same people had been sources of strength and support throughout this ordeal, so I felt an inkling of a duty to explain our reasoning to them. Online community blurs the lines of who we are obligated to include when sharing information. As our case dragged on and on and on, I became less open about *everything,* often choosing to shoot out a Facebook live and calling it good because I didn't have the energy to share all the things with all the people. In an effort to be open and honest, I was not doing a great job of stewarding my own trauma and in turn, I was giving people emotional whiplash.

In the end, I was glad that I pulled back a bit regarding when and how I shared information because the pause helped me stay sane, but I do regret not telling our wider community sooner that we were changing the girls' names. In an effort to avoid making this mistake again, I want to explain why we made this decision, controversy and all. Even writing this now, I feel a good deal of trepidation about how this will be received.

Before we were immersed in the world of foster care, I had a secret habit of looking at the profiles of kids who were up for adoption online. I'd scroll through their stories, often crying quietly while the rest of my house slept. Is it odd to be that emotionally attached to strangers? Maybe. Ask me if I care.

I started praying for the kids in the pictures at night before I went to bed. In the morning, I would text Scott pictures of sibling groups and tell him details about their cases. She likes basketball. He likes Marvel movies. They both do well in school. They have trouble making friends. I didn't know these kids, but as we worked toward completing our classes and homestudy, I needed something that kept me grounded in the world of fostering and adoption. I wondered if fostering would allow us to be a part of several children's lives or if we would foster for a short time and then adopt.

One day I sent Scott a picture of a sibling group of five—four boys and one girl. Their profile had been on the site for longer than normal, even for that large number of kids. The girl was deaf, and the profile said that the adopting family would need to have at least one parent proficient in American Sign Language. That was probably the reason. I watched their profile for weeks, and then one day their picture was gone. I wondered who adopted them.

Another sibling group of four boys caught my eye. They were all conventionally handsome, their hair neatly trimmed. The picture showed them together in matching plaid shirts. The oldest was holding a football with his free arm over the next oldest's shoulder. The two little guys were still holding on to a little baby fat, clear brown skin with bright brown eyes. Their names were listed, and all of the boys had F names except one. The three F names were solidly western if a little old soulish, and then the baby was named Spyder. I laughed out loud. What happened there?

Around the same time, some dear Air Force friends of ours were completing an international adoption. They traveled to Lithuania to meet their son who was living in an orphanage. He was not quite two years old, and he spent most of his days lying flat in a crib. He was severely developmentally delayed. Chris and Ali learned that he had been dropped at the orphanage when his parents' doctor suggested they would not want to care for him because of his Down Syndrome diagnosis. One of his caretakers had given him a name.

When they brought their new baby boy home to Florida, they legally changed his name. He would have an "E" name just like his older sister and brother. Ali wrote a lengthy blog post for those of us following their story, outlining their conflict, discussion, and resolution for changing his name. In adoption circles, there is a lot of disagreement about whether name changes should happen or not. People have strong feelings. With older kids, sometimes the children *want* to change their names, while others would never consider it.

With younger children, particularly in the under two crowd, the issue is largely about the adoptive parents, not the adopted kids. Talk to ten adoptive parents, and you will get ten different opinions about how this should be handled. In talking with adult adoptees, I have also gotten an array of stories about how they felt about name changes. For transracial adoptees in white families, some are grateful for names that ground them in their second culture, while others feel name changes are a denial of their first culture. One friend, who was adopted as a baby, asked to have her legal name changed back to her birth name after learning more of her history. Her adoptive parents fully supported this decision because ultimately the people whose opinion matters the most are those children who have been given many names.

Long before the girls became ours, I wrestled with this idea in part because of Chris and Ali's experience and in part because if I adopted a child named Spyder, would I really want to saddle him with that name for the rest of his life? If I changed his name to Charles, would that ruin his chances of becoming a world-renowned tattoo artist?

All joking aside, the names we give our children are important. Sacred even. When we chose names for Will and Ben, we wanted strong, one-syllable first names because I liked the way they sounded with our last name. We chose family names—Hanford and Russell, respectively—for their middle names because we wanted them to carry a piece of our history with them. We also joked that we were setting them up for varied successes. Will Johnson and Ben Johnson sound like pitchers. Will Hanford Johnson and Ben Russell Johnson sound like supreme court justices. W. H. Johnson and B. R. Johnson sound like accomplished authors.

Scott and I had several conversations about whether or not we should change the girls' names. Emma was so young when she came to us, and it became evident fairly early on that reunification was not going to happen. In our kids' generation on my dad's side of the family, there were only four cousins before the girls came. One of them was named Emma, so we felt settled in giving Baby Emma the name we had reserved for a girl when I was pregnant with both boys. Scott was more hesitant than me—he was uncomfortable with the way he felt about taking away a part of her history, but in the end, we decided she would be Case Adrian. Case was Scott's grandmother's maiden name and his sister's middle name. There was something poetic about carrying a name from last to middle to first. Her middle name would be Adrian, a nod to a Jaden Jennings song about leaving a legacy without fear. If Emma was ours forever, she would receive the name we'd put on the shelf for years.

We wrestled with changing Faith's name a little longer. She was older when she came to us—almost eighteen months. Her case was also up in the air much longer, so we knew there was the possibility of her never being ours to name either way. If she did get to stay with us, we didn't want her to be the only child out of four without a name from us. I felt strongly about how a name is the first gift I gave my biological children outside of rental space in my womb. If the girls were going to be ours forever, giving them names felt like an important part of the psychological bonding for me. Until the day our case changed to an adoption track, we called her both Faith and Bea. She answered to both. Once we knew she was staying with our family, we resolved to change her name legally to Bea Marie.

Bea came from my great-grandmother, a bird of a woman with a difficult early life. By the time I was in the picture, she was a tiny cartoon of an old lady. She wore her hair parted on the side with a tiny clip. When we visited her, I'd sit on the floor playing with a jelly jar of pennies she'd saved for me to take home while my parents talked to her about the weather. I explored her little house like a private detective, stealing butter mints from candy dishes in every room. Her given name was Isabel, but everyone called her Bea. Faith's given middle name was already Marie, which happens to be my mom's and my middle name, and I loved that she would have something that tied her at once to her first mom, my mom, and me.

At the root of changing children's names is the issue of what the change represents. If not handled appropriately, it could be seen as a denial of their history, something we were acutely sensitive about. With young children, particularly under the age of two, most people agree that a name change will not have a significant impact. With other children, most people agree that the child should be empowered to keep or change their name. In the instances where a child comes from a significantly different cultural heritage than his or her adoptive family, an argument can be made for keeping something that signifies that culture and provides a link to his or her past. In my late night prayer sessions, I prayed for several weeks for a set of sisters online, one of whom was named Tequila. I could not in good conscience imagine keeping that name forever, but the reality is that every adoptive parent has to make the best decision at that moment.

Facebook: August 9, 2017
Sister turns 2 on Saturday. Will turns 12 on September 6th.
Baby turns 1 on September 8th.
I came to Target to buy Will some size large gym shorts (the only thing he really needs for back to school), and I decided to look for one small thing for each of them for their birthdays.
And now I'm sobbing in the book aisle at Target because all of my kids are going to college and getting married one day.
#parenting #allthefeelings #iblinked

People often use the varied stories of spiritual name changes in the Bible as an argument for changing names. Abram became Abraham. Sarai became Sarah. Jacob is Israel. Saul is Paul. Simon is Peter. Each of these stories involves a reason for the change—that the lives of these people are taking a different direction. I think it's important to note that in the telling of these stories, we still know their original names. Making a change does not mean what happened before goes away—it means we're going in a different direction.

In the end, we decided that given the aggregate of our approach to adoption, changing their names was okay. If we were planning to hide the fact that they were adopted or never have contact with their biological families, this would be different, but we were walking into the new normal with arms wide open. With intentional effort, we were building relationships with their first parents and reaching out to extended family members because we've learned so much from other adoption stories about best practices.

Is having an open adoption harder? In some ways, yes. Will it serve our girls better in the future? We can't predict what will happen, but based on anecdotal evidence, we think so. As the girls get older, their questions evolve, and I feel strongly about giving them correct and kind answers. I have read stories about and talked with adoptees of all ages, and the ones who know little to nothing about their pasts seem to struggle so much more.

One of my mom's friends found out in middle age that she was adopted and learned that her biological parents and siblings had all lived in the same small town her entire life. This news was devastating as she wrestled with feelings about unanswered questions.

Nicole Chung wrote a beautiful memoir, *All You Can Ever Know*, about her adoption story. Adopted by white parents but of Korean descent, she wrestled with coming to terms with this split culture. When she was pregnant with her first child, she pursued getting answers about her birth family. That journey led her to some ugly truths but also a healing relationship with one of her biological siblings. Chung writes, "Today, when I'm asked, I often say that I no longer consider adoption—individual adoptions, or adoption as a practice—in terms of right or wrong. I urge people to go into it with their eyes open, recognizing how complex it truly is; I encourage adopted people to tell their stories, our stories, and let no one else define these experiences for us."

Overall, I know that eventually the girls will have a better understanding of their stories, and we have committed to never standing in the way of truth, ugly or otherwise. They know their original names, and when they asked why we changed their names, we told them that we chose their names carefully in the same way we chose their brothers' names. We told them that we thought long and hard about what we wanted to call them, that their names connect them to their family and have meaning. Their given names are not a secret, and sometimes we overhear them playing with baby dolls named Faith and Emma.

One time during a car ride when Bea was seven, she said, "Can you call me Faith sometimes?" And I told her yes. The next day she said she wanted to be Bea again. We cannot predict what questions they will have, what will trigger trauma-based actions and reactions, what will make them angry or confused or hurt, but I've learned from my adopted friends that staying open and honest is the best starting point.

CHAPTER ELEVEN
The Calling

Facebook: September 14, 2017

Things the baby has eaten this week: cardboard, paper, dog food, fake grass, the rubber casing off a nunchuck, real grass, part of a board book, and possibly a bead. If I could, I would post a picture from every time I swoop her up and dig things out of her mouth, but since I can't, please know that her face reads: I REGRET NOTHING.

#fostercare #babygirl #teething #alsoeatsfood

When people ask me why I became a foster parent, there is an undercurrent to this simple question. They want to know where the idea came from, and I believe their motivation is rooted in two kinds of soil. Either the idea is new and/or inconceivable to them, or they have already been thinking about becoming a foster parent, too.

As these conversations grow, I've found that most people land in the first camp. For whatever reason, they've never met a foster parent before, and if they've picked up any impression from pop culture along the way, they believe fostering is either an arduous, painful process full of heartbreak or a means to adoption. These assumptions are fair, but they are, like most assumptions, an incomplete picture.

The ones who land in the second camp—these are the people who continue to probe, to ask more specific questions, who insert drifting sentences into the conversation. *I've thought about fostering, but ...*

When I find myself in these conversations with people who want to know more because there is some kind of niggling feeling in the back of their throat that might give way to tears or confessions of deep heart desires, my first reaction is to tell them this: despite appearances, I did not actually feel *called* to foster care. The calling was much broader than that, and foster care was one avenue that allowed me to live out my calling.

I grew up in the evangelical church during the 1980s and 90s where the concept of finding your calling seemed to be the hero's journey. I spent Sunday mornings at the altar (and Sunday nights at Bible study and Wednesday nights at youth group and the occasional Friday night at prayer meetings) searching for inspiration and meaning. I found kindred spirits among the Old Testament characters who heard God's voice (sometimes audibly) telling them to complete great feats. Abraham would be fruitful and multiply. Rahab would protect the spies. Esther had perfect timing. Isaiah volunteered wholeheartedly to go wherever God sent him. This all felt right and good, and I knew that God would call me from inside a burning bush or write me a letter on my bedroom wall. I was convinced.

As I navigated adolescence, I began to understand calling in a somewhat rigid sense. She was called to be a pastor. He was called to be a teacher. She was called to be a doctor. For a child with perfectionist tendencies, I was relieved to learn that the New Testament exhortation to "be perfect" really meant to be complete and to be who God created me to be. What freedom I felt in knowing that everything God required of me was already a part of who I am.

My college years were at the height of Rick Warren's popularity, when literally millions of people (and not just those in the American evangelical club) were searching for a way to live a purpose-driven life.

His book really was transformative for a lot of people in shifting their focus from finding a very specific path to understanding that all of life was purposeful.

As my faith evolved, I became acquainted with the work of Frederick Buechner and learned that my calling was where my passions would meet the world's greatest needs. In recent years, I saw an interview where Stephen Colbert talked about how his job has never felt like a job because when you are doing what you are passionate about, it doesn't feel like work. When you feel intimately connected to your life's purpose, even the hard stuff feels joyful.

One of the things that has always defined my life is that I'm drawn to challenging systems of injustice. In second grade, my friends and I spent our free time creating intricate paper earrings. Our private school dress code only allowed post-style earrings, so we circumvented the rule by cutting out colorful paper designs and wore them with the posts stuck through the paper. Very fancy. When one of the club members decided to exclude one of my friends for some unknown mean girl reason, I stole the stash of paper earrings and ripped them to pieces. If everyone wasn't invited, the club was over.

I'd like to think my tactics have evolved over time, but if I was to pinpoint my actual calling in the evangelical sense of the word, my goal is this: to love everyone and to right wrongs. That has taken many forms over the years: standing up to grade school bullies, civic engagement at both the local and national levels, instilling the values of kindness and inclusion in the hearts of my children, and funding programs through my nonprofit that empower women and communities worldwide. When I became a foster parent, it was not because I was called specifically to "minister to" kids in care or to address issues within the system. I felt that foster care was a perfect avenue to love people and right wrongs.

In a sense, I believe at least for people of faith, this calling belongs to all of us. When Jesus was asked to name the greatest commandment, he said we were to love God and love people. If there is a running theme to the way Jesus lived his life, it's that he did stuff a lot of people wouldn't do and called out injustices as he saw them. He didn't knock over tables because he had anger management issues. He knocked over tables because religious leaders were taking advantage of people. He didn't invite the religious elite into his inner circle. He asked fishermen and tax collectors and (*gasp!*) women because he wanted people who were more interested in loving people than being right or having a shiny image. He spent most of his time talking to and healing people everyone else shunned—lepers, prostitutes, people from other ethnic groups—because he recognized this was the center of God's heart.

I would need to write another book to lament how sad I am to see what the Western church has done to Jesus' message, but every time I'm tempted to completely throw in the towel, I'm reminded that Jesus wept before he raised Lazarus from the dead. I'm remind-ed that he met the physical needs of the 5,000. I'm reminded that he encouraged his followers to be like children. His ministry was full of vulnerability and practicality and simplicity, and that's the Jesus I love and try to emulate. I also act like him a lot when I'm tired and don't want to be around people. Praise be to the introvert messiah.

I'm just going to be honest. In the current climate, I'm hesitant to start any sentence with "The Bible says ..." because so many of my evangelical counterparts are using those words to encase hate-filled arrows they then fling toward people who disagree with them. So when I say this, I want to be clear about my intentions. I am going to write about some things that the Bible says and then tell you what those things mean to me. Later, I will need you to back me up when people who haven't read my book call me a heretic or give me a one star review because women—especially one who has never been to seminary—shouldn't be trusted with exegesis. (See, I really need to write that other book. Or go to more therapy.)

In the book of James, the Bible says that "Pure and genuine religion in the sight of God the Father means caring for orphans and widows in their distress and refusing to let the world corrupt you" (1:27, *NLT*). In foster care, I am able to take this admonition quite literally. These children are in distress, and I get to be a safeguard for their well-being. More broadly, I believe this scripture speaks to caring for anyone in our lives who is vulnerable. During the time when this scripture was written, so much of survival relied on a male head of household providing for the needs of children and women, so in that particular society, women and children whose husbands and fathers were gone were vulnerable. That's still the case for so many women and children around the world. This is why I spent years working to empower women through access to healthcare, education, economic empowerment, and safety in nonprofit spaces.

In modern-day America, some of our most vulnerable are kids in care and other children living in poverty, people experiencing homelessness, and people with physical and/or mental health disabilities. I could sit here all day and come up with other categories of people who fit the "vulnerable" descriptor. The point is that if we take our "religion" seriously as the book of James describes it, we need to take care of our neighbors who are suffering without support.

The second part of that verse has always been interesting to me because more often than not in sermons I've heard about being "in the world and not of the world" and "refusing to let the world corrupt" me, the focus has always been on personal behaviors. The problem with this is the slippery slope into a ridiculous amount of legalism and judgment. The list of Things Good Christians Do Not Do is long, and as a young person it was hard to keep up with where the okay/not okay line was.

I remember having sincere conversations with friends and adults about whether or not my clothes would cause my brothers in Christ to sin or whether I needed to repent for watching an R-rated movie. I specifically remember sitting in a prayer room at the church with a friend who had sex with her boyfriend of three years. She was weeping with shame because she felt as though she had allowed the world to corrupt her. I comforted her and assured her that God still loved her. Now as an adult, this framework that adult leaders set up for us is so troubling. It makes me angry that there was ever a question in her mind or mine as to whether God would love us because of any of these things.

When I read that verse and others that tell me to refuse to let the world corrupt me, this is how I hear that now: God has called us to love people and to care for the vulnerable. When we lose sight of that because we are distracted by things that are not God's heart, we are corrupt. Chasing selfish ambition at the expense of others, turning a blind eye to people who are hurting—these actions are the fruit of a corrupted heart, not whether I watched the latest Oscar winner or drank one too many glasses of wine.

I am not a seminary-trained theologian with a flock of congregants. I decided a long time ago that was not the path I would take to live out my calling despite several mentors suggesting I'd make a good pastor. It's kind of like how people are always wanting Oprah to run for political office. Oprah and I are the same—we feel honored by the suggestion and will continue to politely decline. (Years from now, if Oprah breaks our pact and becomes president, I'm still not going to be a pastor.)

However, I do feel as if being a part of the fostering community has allowed me to shepherd a good number of people in the right direction—from friends who have become foster parents to our kids' biological family members to the children I'm raising in my home. Fostering has revealed the depth of God's love like nothing else for me. The experience has given me the opportunity to love people unconditionally in ways that can only be supernatural and has steeled my resolve to seek justice. Loving people and righting wrongs—that's what I'm doing, and because I know this is exactly what I'm supposed to be doing, I persevere through every hard thing and consider it pure joy.

CHAPTER TWELVE
THE SEARCH

Facebook: October 10, 2017
"Every time someone's told me something was going to be really hard,
it hasn't been that hard … I study, I train—it's not that hard. I think
this finally might be the thing that's as hard as everyone says it is."
"It's only been three hours."
Randall and Beth are the reason I watch every week.
#thisisus

After several conversations with Jessica via text and in person, I determined that she got pregnant sometime in June, and she believed Chad
was the father. I was suspicious because that was also during the time that
she was living with Don. Following Don's criminal court case findings,
she had to leave his apartment and find somewhere else to live. I tried to
check in regularly because I wanted to make sure she was safe. In the fall,
she moved in with her uncles, two people I'd never met but who seemed
stable. They had a nice, simple house not far from where we lived, and
they had taken in Jessica's younger sister, who had just had her first baby.

As Jessica's belly grew with Baby #5, so did our relationship. We
began texting regularly. We saw each other more frequently. A few

times, I "supervised" visits when the case assistant was unavailable or if we were making up for a missed visit that was not Jessica's fault. I bought her prenatal vitamins and helped her get to a few appointments. She started a job at a restaurant in the mall and was making some money, so she was doing a better job of bringing supplies for the girls to her visits. Most of her visits happened in the restaurant while she was working, so they ate french fries and chicken fingers at every visit. She made sure to tell me that she was trying to give them lemonade instead of soda. Our conversations were often candid. Jessica shared things about her life that troubled me, and I worked hard at listening without reacting and empathizing without judging.

Jessica was always open about her drug use, her history with men, and other problematic family issues. I wanted her to feel like I was a trustworthy counselor, but I also needed to create healthy boundaries for everyone involved. I tried to ask questions to better understand the situation, but I'm sure there were times when my questions felt overbearing and invasive. In the back of my mind, I understood intellectually that our dynamic would always feel a little strained, a little tentative. However, I can say there was never a time I regretted reaching out and inviting her into our world.

From the beginning, it was important to me to leave the door open—we were not just fostering these girls. We were fostering their family, too. I knew there was an opportunity to love her in a way that she may not have ever experienced, and modeling healthy relationships with men and good parenting was something that felt purposeful and natural. In addition to the impact I knew building that bridge would have on Jessica, I wanted to be able to tell the girls in the future anything they wanted to know about their first mom. My hope was that our relationship would always be open and that the truth would set everyone free.

Throughout the first months of Jessica's pregnancy, she seemed excited and motivated. Every time we were together, she asked questions about our family, ranging from general curiosity to haltingly personal.

Where did we grow up? What was college like for me? Did I become a foster parent because I couldn't have any more kids? I answered truthfully, recognizing that the more time Jessica spent with us, she was becoming more comfortable and more conflicted, perhaps in equal measures. I know because she said things out loud like "I could never give the girls the life you give them!" and "I'll never give up. I'm going to keep trying to get them back."

Whenever she talked about getting the girls back, I tried to be supportive, but from what I knew, she was getting closer and closer to having her rights terminated. She was not meeting the requirements of her service plan, and I wasn't sure if she really understood what was going on. When I talked to our new case manager, Marcus, he told me again and again that he had had conversations with her about what she needed to be doing. The fact that she was not completing her service plan but still talking about getting the girls back led me to believe she didn't understand the process. Again, this is the tension of foster care—trying to be supportive and honest without giving false hope. In November, he told us that he would be filing a legal screen on Emma/Case.

A legal screen is the process that starts parental termination. The case manager fills out a load of paperwork that includes information from nine measurable months. If during those nine months, parents are found to be unsatisfactory, the state can move forward with termination. Because Chad had disappeared completely, and Jessica was not executing her service plan, Marcus felt the legal screen would pass. I took this information with a grain of salt because nothing in foster care is real until it is. Marcus explained that he would file the paperwork, and we would probably find out after the New Year if the screen had passed. He was not filing a legal screen on Faith/Bea because Don's involvement was satisfactory. He was making his two hour weekly visits, and he was executing the other requirements on his service plan.

As we got closer to Christmas, Jessica seemed to pull away from me gradually. I'm not sure if this drift was noticeable at the time, or if I am just working with the benefit of hindsight. I continued to try to have touchpoints with her. She became increasingly disinterested in interacting with the girls, either as a natural consequence of seeing them more with our family or because of other underlying issues. For Christmas, she spent her entire paycheck on gifts for the girls and her two boys who were living with Don. Trying to explain to her that saving that money for something more important was pointless. At one point, she told me she self-reported when the case manager asked her to take a random drug test, which confirmed my suspicions.

I found myself in an awkward position—I wanted to continue to be a part of Jessica's life for many reasons, but I had to consider if her interaction with the girls was good for them. I also had to consider how to handle knowing that she was using drugs while pregnant. Our relationship had developed to the point that I felt like I could say things to her like "You can't do drugs while you're pregnant" without risking her shutting down. So I did. And she was relatively receptive.

Because Case was born drug-exposed and Jessica was not making significant progress on her service plan, we knew the state would take this new baby at the hospital. The case manager was discreet and measured in answering our questions, but because we were caring for the baby's siblings, we would be considered first when the state needed to find a home for the new baby. Somewhere in there we found out that Jessica was having another girl.

Will, our child who most resembles Spock from Star Trek, had repeatedly argued that four long-term kids was the best limit for our family. He argued that Scott and I had four hands to hold. He argued that he liked the symmetry of two boys and two girls. He argued that he and Ben each had a little sister to care for. Scott was leaning in this direction as well. Without saying so, I think Scott was committed to quietly taking the temperature of our whole family, and in times when I lacked clarity for self-preservation, he offered a gentle voice of reason. Like many times in our life together, Scott played the role of a firefighter intent on containing my flames before they got out of hand. Even if I felt like my heart could expand to include more kids, I knew taking this new baby was not prudent.

As if that wasn't enough to consider, Scott found out he would be moving on military orders the next summer. We already knew there was a good chance that our case would still be open, and our family would be geographically separated for some period of time until a permanency goal was reached. Scott did not have a choice about when the Air force would move him, but there wasn't a single second that we considered anything but staying committed to seeing this case to its end. Scott would move to Washington state, and the rest of us would live in Illinois, and we had no idea how long we would maintain this status.

In his beautiful novel, *Extremely Loud and Incredibly Close*, Jonathan Safran Foer narrates from the perspective of a nine-year-old boy named Oskar Schell who lost his father in the 9/11 attacks. Since reading the book years ago, I have quoted Oskar many times when I find myself feeling sad. Oskar describes his grief and the collective sadness of New York City as wearing "heavy boots." He talks about avoiding his father's room for a full year after his death but then finally putting on his heavy boots to walk into a room full of triggering memories. That's what it felt like when I told the case manager we weren't going to be able to take the baby full-time. I wore heavy boots for weeks. I wore them around the house. I wore them to pick up the kids from school. I wore them to bed. I couldn't shake the feeling like we were failing this baby by separating her from her siblings, but I also knew that our family had to know our capacity.

One of the hardest parts of fostering for me has been knowing what my job is and isn't. I know I have a commanding personality. I know I can be intimidating to other people. I wanted to start the conversation with Marcus without him feeling like I was questioning his ability to do his job well. In the middle of our case, I knew that Marcus was an exceptional case manager. Of course, there were times when we miscommunicated about something or when I had a different opinion than he did about something, but overall, I recognized how hard he was hustling. In talking to other foster parents about some pretty significant horror stories, I felt even more grateful for Marcus' role in our story.

I sat on my feelings for a while before telling Marcus that we knew we would not be able to add another child to our family, but I didn't leave him hanging. I asked what we could do to prepare for the baby's arrival. So much of foster care feels last minute and fly-by-the-seat-of-your-pants. There was no reason for that to be the case in finding a family for this baby. I expressed to him how strongly we felt about finding the right family who would be open to having a relationship with us, too. Marcus welcomed my input—a nice change of pace for once—as having a bond between our family and the new family would only benefit everyone. After she arrived, we would be asked to facilitate sibling visits, and that would work better if everyone was on the same page.

Word was out that a baby was coming, and I started getting messages from friends and strangers. Now, I mean this in the nicest way—I love that so many people are willing to adopt. What was frustrating about this process is that I had half a dozen people tell me they "felt led" to reach out. The problem is that none of those people "felt led" to do the work of preparing for an adoption. We were on a timeline. DCFS was not going to give a baby to some random nice family. I needed someone who had actually done the work. Ideally, that someone would be licensed through the same agency, so all the children involved could have the same caseworker. That narrowed the field significantly.

Scott and I were part of a foster parent support group at the time, and we met once a month. Shortly after my conversation with Marcus, we had a meeting, and I thought maybe I could scout out the room for someone who fit the criteria. In a cosmically hilarious moment that Friday night, I looked around and every family in the room including us was already fostering a baby, or the woman in the family was pregnant. Some of them were both pregnant *and* fostering a baby. I laughed a little, but mostly, I felt like I was just going to keep fielding non-contenders, and then the baby was going to end up going to a random house. What if that family lived far away making it too difficult for us to have sibling visits? What if they weren't open at all to a relationship with us?

The next week, the girls and I were at their weekly gymnastics class. One of the other moms, Jamalyn, knew our story because we'd been chatting every Wednesday for the last couple of months while our kids balanced on beams and swung from bars. I shared with her my frustrations, noting that the baby was due at the end of February. This was a couple of weeks before Christmas, and we had no prospects.

Facebook: October 16, 2017
I started singing directions this morning to get the babies to stop fussing and listen ("It's time to put on our socks!") and now every time I try to talk in a normal voice, Sister holds up her hands and yells, "STOP, Mommy! Sing!"
So I sing. Everything.
#tinydictator #fostercare #babygirls #momlife

Jamalyn told me she knew a friend of a friend who was getting licensed. She added that she knew the woman, but they weren't super close friends or anything. She also knew nothing about which agency they were with or anything else significant. Jamalyn had seen Kelly talking about foster care on Facebook and said she would connect us.

On December 20th of 2017, I got a message from Kelly detailing where their family was in the process. They were licensed through the right agency, and because of their bedroom set up, they were looking to accept a baby girl. Kelly's message was warm and unassuming. At the end of her message she said they were happy to help if I thought their family was a good fit. Before messaging her back, I stalked her Facebook profile for a bit like any normal person would. Not much was public, but I was able to see that she was married with three kids, two boys and a girl. One of the only public posts on her page was a call to her community to help a locally owned restaurant that had caught fire. She was asking her people to show up for meals now that the restoration was done, so the couple who owned the restaurant would know the community cared about them. That's how I knew Kelly was my person. I wasn't looking for someone who just signed up to be a foster parent. I was looking for someone who lived kindness and goodness in every area of her life. I messaged her back immediately, answering a few questions she'd asked.

We were two days away from leaving for a ten-day trip over Christmas to visit friends and family in Missouri and Oklahoma. My message back to her included some key information: we were still up in the air about whether or not we were taking in the baby; we wanted a family that understood the importance of siblings being able to know each other; and our family might be moving the next summer on military orders. Kelly shared that her sister had adopted twin girls a few years before, and the whole family grieved that they weren't connected with their biological siblings because the other families had opted for closed adoptions. If I needed any more confirmation that we were headed in the right direction, that was it.

We agreed to circle back after the holidays, so we could meet in real life. Until then, we would pray about the decision and talk to our people.

Facebook: November 29, 2017
Petroleum jelly is totally non-toxic, right? Not asking for a friend. I went pee and came out to a baby painting herself and sampling Vaseline. *#help #babyrebel #futureworldchanger*

CHAPTER THIRTEEN
The Flood

One of the more stressful parts about moving frequently is not knowing what kind of housing options exist in new places. When we moved to Illinois, long before we started fostering, we ended up in a 1930s bungalow by default. We considered living on base, but when that didn't pan out, we expanded our search to the local area. We ruled out a few houses because the rent was too high, and several disappeared out from under us before we could even consider signing a lease. Such is life during PCS season. The schedule of military moves requires a lot of families to have a "permanent change of station" during the summer. It was July, and countless other families were looking for the same kind of house we were.

Scott and I drove by a red brick house with a for rent sign in the yard that had not been listed on any of the websites we'd been scouring. We parked and entered the house to find a man in a splattered shirt and pants who informed us he was the painter, not the owner. We asked some clarifying questions, and he told us the previous renters had been in the house for several years, and the owner was doing some rehab to get the property ready to sell or rent again. We thanked him for his time and left.

Scott and I discussed the pros and cons of living in an older home versus a standard move-in ready option. Our decision to move into this house was heavily swayed by the fact that the rent was about two-thirds of any of the other options we'd seen. We had a trip planned to OK to visit family and friends, so Scott got to work arranging for our household goods to be delivered after we returned from OK and some repairs were finished.

Two weeks later, we started unpacking. I marveled at the original tile work in the downstairs bath. All of the doorknobs and light fixtures were ornate, something from a movie where an unsuspecting child might open a door into Wonderland. The floors creaked with the sounds of good but old bones.

We took to calling the house Garden Manor, given its placement on a road named Garden Boulevard. Like all old homes, it had quirks. A random door in a wall that served no purpose. Pull cord lighting in tiny closets. Outer doors with a confusing number of keys to manage. Of all its quirks, the plumbing seemed most baffling. We wondered who had done the work several times as the basement flooded easily, something characteristic of many houses in southern Illinois. We learned about the increasing problem of soil erosion in the area and the importance of sump pumps for the first time. We talked with the property manager multiple times about our concerns with the way the pipes were shoddily pieced together. Twice, a restoration company had to come in with machines to suck up water from the basement and giant fans to air out the moisture.

In December of 2017, we celebrated a year of fostering. Emma/Case seemed to be moving toward termination, and Faith/Bea's case was wide open. We asked Santa to visit our house a few days early and then set off again for ten days in Missouri and Oklahoma to visit our friends and family for Christmas. After making multiple stops, each visit adding to a mountain of gifts for our four kids, we headed home to Illinois on New Year's Eve with a car that would have made the Clampetts beam with pride. My parents had traveled and arrived back at Garden Manor with us in the early evening.

My dad entered the house first, and I heard him say, "Uh oh."

I was a few feet behind, dragging a suitcase through the kitchen, and assumed something small had happened. Maybe the Christmas tree had fallen over in our absence, weighed down by our growing collection of ornaments. Instead, I walked through the doorway to the dining room to find the walls caving in. Beyond the table, still decorated with a festive red tablecloth and candy bowls, I could see a waterfall in the living room. A steady rush of water flowed directly onto our bloated leather couch. Beneath sheetrock and plaster, I could see many of the presents we'd left stacked neatly on the floor from our celebration before we left on our trip.

My dad and Scott went into recovery mode immediately, searching for and shutting off the water main. I made a mental list of all the people we needed to call. Property manager, insurance company, caseworker. My mom shuffled the kids upstairs after we assessed that the damage was confined to the bottom story. It was close to the end of the business day on New Year's Eve, so I will be eternally grateful for the way I was treated by each person who answered my phone calls.

Thankfully, returning from a ten-day trip meant we had at least a week's worth of clothing for everyone in our suitcases, not to mention the mountain of gifts from our friends and family. My parents took the kids to their house, bathed the girls, and ordered pizza, while Scott and I stayed behind to meet with the restoration company who miraculously sent someone out within hours of finding the damage.

Illinois was experiencing one of its coldest winters on record, so we were not the only people dealing with burst pipes. We had followed all conventional wisdom and left the heat on in our absence, but the 5° high for the day was enough to freeze the aging plumbing anyway. Later, the insurance company and other contractors would tell us that pipes had burst in multiple places and that there was nothing we could have done to avoid what happened.

After assessing what we could, we were advised to leave the house as-is because asbestos testing would need to be done. Because the flood had affected the electricity, the house was measuring 10° within hours of our arrival and a thin layer of ice covered the windows and floors.

I snapped some pictures of the damage and walked out unsure about when we would be back in the house to salvage our things. I felt oddly comforted when we were told that the freeze would probably help keep the mold at bay for a little while. Our friends, Josh and Amanda, saw the pictures I posted on Facebook and ordered us to come to their house for dinner. They had already planned on grabbing McDonald's, so they added food for us to their order. We drove a couple of miles to their house and sank into their dining room chairs for french fries.

I emailed the caseworker and told him we had an emergency. He called me, and I filled him in. He said to just keep him in the loop because we would need to fill out the paperwork for our new address.

Scott called housing at the base and learned they had availability in a TLF. Temporary Lodging Facilities are hotel rooms and full-sized houses designed to house military families if they need short-term stays. They are a godsend to many of us who use them on one end or the other of a cross-country move as a cushion. Sometimes household goods have to be moved days or weeks before a family is ready to move, and sometimes a family needs a week in a TLF to find housing at a new base. The TLF available was not pet-friendly, so my parents agreed to keep our dog, Bokonon, for us until we could find another option. We drove to pick up the girls, who would stay with us in the TLF, and the boys were happy to stay with Mimi and Papa and the dog for the night.

It was late—hours after the girls would normally have been in bed, and the weather was bitterly cold. Our first TLF had a loud beeping noise coming from a panel we found under a stairwell, and as it was a holiday, maintenance was spread thin and no one knew how to turn it off. Luckily, another room was available, so we drove down the road a bit and bundled two babies in blankets and footie pajamas into our new "home." By the time we settled them in their pack and plays, it was almost midnight, and all we could do was laugh. Scott and I sat together on the hotel bed, each of us on a device trying to work out some element of this logistical nightmare.

A few minutes later, Will called. When we had first walked into the mess, he had a less than gracious preteen response—something along the lines of how with no electricity, he would not be able to play his video games. I snapped at him about how it would be helpful if he could look at the big picture. He wanted to say goodnight and added, "Sorry I didn't have the right perspective on things earlier." I assured him everything was going to be okay and that his outburst was forgiven. Good Lord in heaven, we should all be allowed to freak out a bit in the middle of chaos and know that our people are going to love us still. If the last year had taught me anything, it was that in my fallibility, I am saved by the grace of other people's unending kindness.

Scott and I stayed up until midnight for the sake of saying we did and welcomed 2018 as weary, ragged travelers in need of rest.

CHAPTER FOURTEEN
The New Home

We started 2018 in a flurry of trying to find a new place to live. We were hesitant but hopeful that our case would be moving toward completion in enough time to all move together to Washington that summer. After searching for short-term rentals, we understood pretty quickly that our options near the Garden Manor were limited. We were living in a four-bedroom TLF on Scott AFB, and the housing office had been more than accommodating. We realized our best bet was to look for a long-term solution on base.

Scott and I went to the housing office and explained the situation. They were empathetic and didn't bat an eye when we said we weren't exactly sure how long we would need the house with the details of our case up in the air. One of the benefits of living on base is that the people in charge are used to plans changing, so we signed the papers with their promise that if our situation changed, there would be no penalty for breaking the one-year lease.

The only house available at the time was a four-bedroom above our pay grade. When they asked if that was going to work for us, I asked with a laugh, "Is it not flooded? Because that is my only standard at the moment."

Scott got to work settling the logistics of scheduling movers to get what we could salvage out of Garden Manor. Once we were cleared to go in after the insurance companies had done all their assessments, a group of guys from his office helped us move some necessities before the moving company would bring the rest later. On a Saturday morning, several men I'd never met showed up with trucks ready to bring the washer and dryer and our beds. We spent the weekend moving things from the TLF and the flooded house into what would be our new home for the foreseeable future.

In the middle of the chaos, families from Zion Lutheran School where our boys attended sent messages saying there were casseroles waiting in the school kitchen for us to pick up when we came to collect the boys. Friends and family members from all over sent cash through Paypal and care packages to my parents' house while we weren't sure what address to use. Other military friends with base access dropped off gift cards to Target and fast food restaurants. I have said this one million times—there is no greater ministry than the ministry of food when everything feels terrible. For the middle two weeks of January, we survived on cereal, chicken bakes, and brownies.

Several times I ran out to the BX, the base exchange which is the military equivalent of a department store, to get things we couldn't find—a curtain rod, power strips, cooking utensils. We bought a folding table for the dining room and used another for a TV stand. The new house had an open floor plan with a giant main living area. The boys had pillow fights and wrestling matches while the girls ran circles through the kitchen, dining room, and living room. We made pallets to watch movies on the computer by the fireplace. Living like free-range kids while the temperatures were still below freezing came easy because we didn't have any furniture.

I wondered if the girls were confused by all of the movement. We'd spent ten days in multiple houses traveling for the holidays and moved twice in a span of as many weeks, but they didn't skip a beat. They napped in their pack and plays and crashed at bedtime as if everything was completely normal. They were enamored with the kitchen's mostly empty cabinets which gave way to rousing rounds of hide and seek. I noted in a post on Facebook that at sixteen months, Emma/Case's vocabulary was finally starting to expand. Her new words that week were shoe, poop, and silly. At almost two and a half, Faith/Bea was in full-on little mama mode, nurturing Emma/Case at every turn. Her fierce love for her sister turned into reporting every little thing at all times. "Mommy, baby chew table. Mommy, baby splash toilet. Mommy, baby pull doggy." One day in particular, she made it her mission to sound the alert every time Emma/Case started crying, but her toddlerese came out, "Baby is dying!"

By the end of January, the rest of our household goods arrived, and we started feeling settled. I felt very little loss about most of the things but winced when I thought about how many books were bloated and ruined. My mom texted me a picture she had taken one day when we'd gone in to salvage our stuff. The picture showed a pile of Kurt Vonnegut books, one of which landed open to a page of scrawling text that read "What is the purpose of life?" Her picture made me reflect about how all my Kurt Vonnegut books were dead, but I was inspired by his answer to this question. In *Breakfast of Champions*, Vonnegut says it is "to be the eyes and ears and conscience of the Creator of the Universe, you fool!" In "Sirens of Titans," he says, "A purpose of human life, no matter who is controlling it, is to love whoever is around to be loved." I've settled here: I'm a fool looking for peace of mind and trying to love humans the best I can.

Base living is weird. There's no other way to say it. Every day at 5:00 p.m. the national anthem plays over a loudspeaker. All cars stop driving. People walking their dogs and kids playing basketball in their driveways stop and put their hands over their hearts. The girls caught on quickly, running out to the front porch barefoot in the cold several times. Everywhere we went, Emma/Case screamed "Daddy!" at anyone she saw in uniform. Even the women.

As odd as it sounds, the chaos gave me something else to think about other than how our case was up in the air. I dropped the girls off at my parents one morning, so I could run to Walmart for a big grocery run. My phone rang, and Marcus' words were the first I had heard in the entirety of our case that made me feel hopeful. He said, "I'm calling to let you know the legal screen for Emma passed."

"Okay, and that means ..." I said tentatively.

"That means that we will ask for her permanency goal to be changed at the next court date," he explained. "Instead of reunification, she'll be listed as substitution care pending termination."

Words have meanings, but at that moment nothing meant anything. My brain was firing off questions faster than I could put them into words. I said, "I think I know what that means, but can you explain it more?"

Marcus laughed a little. "Yes, so at the next permanency hearing, I'll testify that the legal screen passed, and we will move forward to terminate parental rights."

"And then we can adopt her?" I asked.

"As long as the judge agrees with the findings of the legal screen."

I broke down in the cereal aisle. I literally sat down on the floor in tears, other shoppers giving me concerned looks. I waved them away, cupping my hand over the phone and saying, "It's fine. I'm fine. They're happy tears!"

Marcus went on to explain that Faith/Bea would more than likely stay on a reunification track because Don was making satisfactory progress toward a return home goal. I asked for maybe the tenth time over the last few months if they would increase his hours with her. I wholeheartedly believed that the best plan of action was for her to stay with us forever, but if Don was a viable option, the current plan for her to see him two hours a week and then go back to him was not fair. There had to be a gradual transition for her sake. In our home, she was with her sister. She was eating healthy food and getting enough sleep. She had access to extracurricular activities and other enriching experiences. Don was living in a hotel, ate most of his meals at McDonald's, and had unreliable childcare.

Let me be clear—people in his situation can still be good parents. This is not about comparing our material wealth to his. It's about shifting a child's entire worldview overnight. Because I know of other cases where this transition has happened very suddenly, my biggest immediate worry was that she would not be prepared for this change. Of course, I had more pressing big picture worries about the kind of life she would live as she got older, but I had to shut down those thoughts if I wanted to function.

In that moment of elation of finding out that Emma/Case was going to be ours forever pending the judge's approval, I was also filled with a sense of dread about what this might mean for Faith/Bea. Over the next few weeks, multiple people would suggest getting a lawyer to fight, but that's not how foster care works. The fate of all children in foster care is first in the hands of their biological parents and next in the hands of the judges who have to make decisions based on the evidence. Never mind that she called us mommy and daddy or that she'd been in our home for almost a full year at that point. My job was still to protect and serve her as a child in state custody. That meant supporting the reunification goal even if every fiber in my being believed it was a tragedy.

Marcus assured me that his goal was to see Don's hours increased. I asked more questions, but he answered "I can't tell you that" to most of them. When we hung up the phone, I wiped my face with the lapel of my coat and consulted my shopping list. We still needed toilet paper. I started to dial Scott's number to fill him in when reality hit me like a ton of bricks. Scott's orders were to move in May for training in Oklahoma, and then he would continue to Washington in August. Faith/Bea's case being wide open meant there was no way the rest of us could go with him. I'd spent enough hours thinking about all the possible scenarios that could play out that this news was not a shock to my system. I was ready for the challenge of managing the new normal. My biggest concern was the emotional toll this would take on Scott.

About a week after Marcus' phone call, court went as expected. Marcus testified that Emma/Case's legal screen passed, and her goal was changed to substitution care pending termination. Marcus testified that Don was making satisfactory progress and asked that he be given discretion over visitation, which the judge granted. Visitation hours are court ordered, and giving a case manager discretion means that Marcus could increase or decrease hours as needed to serve everyone involved without having to go back to court to change the order.

During the hearing, Don was given the chance to speak, and we were floored at the words that came out of his mouth. The previous July, he had avoided eye contact with us and screamed at the judge. This time, his words were measured and calm. He still felt the need for everyone in the room to know that he was losing his daughter by no fault of his own, and the judge reminded him that he was in charge of his destiny. We were sitting behind him on a bench reserved for us and other people connected to the case. At one point, Don swiveled in his chair to face us. He looked me straight in the eyes and said, "I want to say this in front of everyone and on the record. The Johnsons are taking excellent care of my baby. When I see her I know that she is safe and cared for, so thank you for taking care of her." And then he swiveled back toward the judge. Scott and I exchanged a shocked glance, and I wiped my sweaty hands on my pants while swallowing a lump in my throat.

Marcus explained to us after the hearing that the termination process involved three court dates. The first date would be in April, and ideally, the subsequent hearings would happen spaced about a month apart. Based on his math, Emma/Case's termination would happen sometime in June. Faith/Bea's case would continue for the next six months until we met again for permanency in July.

As we left the courtroom, Don stood in the hallway waiting to sign papers, and I approached him. The moment felt otherworldly. I noted his worn shoes and pants. He looked exhausted. He was wearing a work shirt with his name on the pocket. Scott and I stood with him for over half an hour. I tried to communicate with him everything I'd been thinking about for the last seven months. I thanked him for what he said in the courtroom and assured him that we were honored to have Faith/Bea in our home. I told him I wished we could have an open line of communication like I had with Jessica because we needed each other, and Faith/Bea would be better off if we all worked together. I was surprised at how receptive he was. He repeatedly thanked us again, his gratefulness peppered with comments about how he was being unfairly treated by the court. He said he was going to fight to the end to get his daughter back. I told him I understood that. I told him that I'd been pushing for her to have more hours with him, and he looked surprised. I told him I didn't want this to take longer than needed because it wasn't fair to Faith/Bea and would only be more confusing to her the longer the case dragged on. He agreed.

Emma/Case was eventually going to be officially ours. While Faith/Bea was in limbo, at least we had opened a door with Don. The day as a whole was a much needed win.

Facebook: January 31, 2018
Four kids at home for the second day in a row—all still functioning at appropriate levels. Did a good amount of work in the kitchen this morning. Took the girls' first mom to her OB appointment (all is well!). Filed our taxes. Ate pecan brownies for breakfast and lunch. So much adulting today already. I should probably reward myself with another brownie.

CHAPTER FIFTEEN
The Grandparents

If the January timeline seems a bit muddled in my story, imagine living it. We were all over the place emotionally and physically, but the strength of our community carried us well. On a sunny Saturday morning, Scott and the kids gathered around our folding table in the dining room. I'd fried bacon and flipped a million pancakes. Case had taken to throwing her hands in the air announcing "SO BIG!" At one point, I snapped a picture of my five favorite people, all of them arms raised in unison over plates in various stages of finished.

I heard my phone ding with an incoming text and went to check. My Aunt Lyn sent a message saying that my grandpa, my dad's dad, was dying. He'd been suffering for a couple of years from alcohol-induced dementia. A lifelong alcoholic and former asbestos worker, we had often marveled at his body's ability to withstand the tests he'd given it. Now it seemed he was in his last stages. We'd seen him over the Christmas break in his memory care unit. The kids each talked to him, and he smiled. For most of his life, Grandpa Dink was reserved at best and hostile at worst. His relationships with his children were complicated. As a child, I observed this dynamic through the lens of innocence. I mostly remembered him for his stories about hunting, the pictures of the years he lived in Alaska working on the pipeline, and for nearly silent walks in the woods on the family farm in Missouri when he would occasionally tell me some tiny fact about a tree's life cycle or some unique quality about a bird native to the Midwest.

When the boys were little, we visited him as often as we could in his log cabin in the woods where he'd settled after my grandparents' divorce. He was still drinking, so our visits were always a bit tentative at first because we didn't know what state of mind he'd be in. Mostly, he was sober enough to be pleasant, and he was gentle with the boys. He'd show them fishing lures he'd fashioned himself, take them on walks to see wildflowers on the back of his property, and let them help him refill his hummingbird feeders. They wore his cowboy hats and raced around his small house. He was mesmerized by their stories about superheroes told in tiny voices. They knew nothing of the tension the adults felt in those moments.

Over time, his behavior became erratic, something indicative of more than alcoholism and after his diagnosis, my dad and his sisters determined he needed to be moved to a facility where professionals could care for him. When Lyn sent the text, I knew I needed to be in Joplin with my extended family. Scott agreed, and I packed my bags and started driving. I got there Saturday night and spent the next day taking turns sitting at his bedside. My dad was in India, but my mom drove down a bit later. Her mom, my Grandma Hazel, was in a different wing of the same facility recovering from a fall. My mom had been making regular trips to Joplin to help her siblings care for my grandma and make arrangements for moving her into a different senior apartment when she was released from rehab.

My aunts, their husbands, and all of the cousins from my generation on my dad's side of the family were gathered in my grandad's room. We ran out to get Sonic and Taco Bell when someone was hungry. We took turns leaving to grab showers at Lyn's house not far from the nursing home. Overnight, I walked the halls back and forth between Grandpa Dink's room and Grandma Hazel's room. Somewhere around 3 a.m.,

I went to my grandma's room. She was asleep in a recliner, which she preferred, and my mom was stretched out in the bed. I woke her up and told her to scoot over, and I slept for a few hours back to back with my mom in a twin-sized hospital bed.

Much of Sunday was spent waiting for nurses to check Grandpa Dink's vitals. His breathing was shallow at times and then sped up at other times. His body was bloated as fluids collected. We dabbed his mouth with a sponge, so it didn't get dry, and we talked to him, holding his hands. He had pristine skin for his age, soft and clear. It was the first time I'd watched someone die. I knew I needed to get home, so Scott could go to work on Monday morning. That evening, as Grandpa Dink's breaths came at longer intervals, I got in the car to drive home. He died sometime after midnight with our family around him.

Before I left, I talked with my Grandma Hazel, greeting visitors from my mom's side of the family as they came and went. My mom planned to stay a few more days until they could get Grandma settled in her new apartment.

Monday morning, I hit the ground running, getting the boys to school and checking off meetings for the girls. My family decided to have a small memorial for my grandpa on Wednesday, so I turned around Tuesday evening with the kids to go back. Family members from out of town drove in, and we celebrated my grandpa's life quietly, gathering at a restaurant for a meal. While we were there, I took the kids to visit my Grandma who had gone home briefly only to be brought back to the nursing home because she was severely dehydrated. My mom told me that Grandma had said over and over that she was ready to die, but she seemed in good spirits as the girls toddled around her room. After the memorial for my grandad, we made the drive back to Illinois and continued working on getting our house unpacked.

Kelly, the woman who had contacted me about being our backup when the baby came, had been communicating on Facebook, and we met once at a Panera to talk about the possibilities. Meeting her in person sealed the deal for me. Later, she would tell me that the meeting felt like I said one million words, and she was just trying to get a handhold in the whirlwind. I told her that we were 99% settled on the idea that the timing was not right for us to take another baby long-term. What we were feeling before Christmas was confirmed by everything that had happened after. When the baby came, she would live with Kelly and her family, and we would navigate a new normal of trying to raise children from the same mother together. We coined the term "foster-in-law" to name what we were about to be. We could figure out the rest later.

Our case manager, Marcus, and Kelly's case manager were on the same page about this plan, and the only hitch would come if the baby came early. Their family had a vacation planned for the first two weeks of February, and the baby was due February 26th. Jessica had had all of her babies early, so the contingency was that we would take the baby if she came while they were in Hawaii, and she would move to their house upon their return.

Jessica was living in a maternity home, communicating with me regularly, and occasionally coming to our house for dinner. At one point, she told me she hadn't eaten in days and proceeded to eat three heaping bowls of chicken noodle soup and half a loaf of bread. That night, her belly swollen to capacity, she helped me bathe the girls and get them to bed. We talked candidly about the fact that there was a good chance that the state was going to take this baby. I'd been counseled to not discuss any of the details about Kelly's involvement, and I felt torn because it felt like I was hiding information from her. I also knew it wasn't my job to give her this information and doing so could both make Marcus' job harder and drive her away. I wanted so badly to make sure Jessica was healthy and that the baby was healthy all the way up until she delivered. I questioned whether she really understood the dynamics at play because she believed if she stayed at the maternity home where she was living, she would be able to keep her baby. I was concerned about her ability to pass a drug test at delivery.

Kelly's family left for Hawaii on February 2nd, and at noon on the 3rd, I got a text from Jessica saying she thought she was in labor. I asked if she wanted me to come get her, and she said she wasn't going to the hospital yet. An hour later, she texted that she was going to the hospital, but her mom was going to take her. I told her to keep me updated. I packed a few things in my purse and went to Target, posting vaguely on Facebook asking people to pray for Jessica. In the four o'clock hour, I got a text with a picture of a fresh newborn. Baby K had arrived in record time. I asked Jessica if she was hungry and drove through Freddy's to get her a burger and fries.

When I got to the hospital, Jessica's mom was leaving. She had to go back to work. I walked into the room with my paper sack of food and found Jessica alone in her bed, the baby in the bassinet beside her. I started to ask if anyone else was there, confused as to why none of Jessica's family members or friends were there not even half an hour after she gave birth. I held my tongue when I saw a smile spread across Jessica's face at the sight of the Freddy's sack.

The two of us sat and talked about K's birth as she ate. K was healthy by all appearances, and Jessica had barely gotten into the delivery room before the baby came out. I asked if I could hold her, and Jessica was happy to oblige while she finished her meal. While I held the baby, a hospital worker brought in a tray of food, and Jessica went to work on that as well. I made a joke about how she had worked up an appetite getting this precious baby into the world.

At one point, a woman who turned out to be a distant cousin showed up, held the baby for a few minutes, and left. Jessica rolled her eyes as the lady left and said, "I don't know why she came. I don't even know her that well. She just saw that K was born on Facebook."

As evening fell, I wasn't sure what the plan was. Jessica said she didn't think any of her family was planning to come back. I asked if she knew if DCFS was coming, and she said she thought so but didn't offer any more information. I asked about Chad, and she said he wouldn't be there. She'd texted him a picture of the baby, and his girlfriend had texted back, "I'm going to kick ur ass now that ur not pregnant I hope your baby dies"

I texted Scott that I'd be home at some point but that I wasn't leaving her here alone. Someone came in to help Jessica get to the bathroom, and I took the opportunity to talk with one of the nurses in the hall. I explained our dynamic and told her I would leave to get some things at my house, but I would be back. I asked if she had any information about DCFS. She told me that both Jessica and the baby had tested positive for cocaine, so an investigator had been called.

Walking back into the room and remaining calm was one of the hardest things I've ever had to do. I told Jessica I was going to run home for some things and would stay the night if she thought that would be helpful. She said, "You can stay if you want to."

"I don't have to stay," I said. "I only want to stay if you want me here. I just don't want you to be alone. Tell me what you want because this is about you. Also, what do you need? Do you have clothes for K? Or pajamas for you so you don't have to stay in a hospital gown?"

She didn't have anything. Not clothes. Not toiletries. Nothing she needed for a hospital stay, so I gave her the layette for K and the pajamas for her I'd brought from Target and told her I could go for more things the next day. She told me she wanted me to stay.

Before I left the hospital, the DCFS investigator showed up and asked if he could talk to me. I filled him in on why I was there and how Jessica was living in a maternity home because she knew it was her best chance at keeping her baby. I told him I wasn't shocked about the positive cocaine test and knew that was a nail in her coffin. In typical foster care fashion, he said he would need to talk with her and with her case manager, but the drug use and the fact that she had an open case with the girls was not going to work in her favor. He was gracious and kind and respectful, as were all the nurses and doctors involved.

I went home to pack an overnight bag and check in with Scott. All four kids had been in bed for hours, and I told him I wasn't sure what the next day would bring. I took a minute to update Kelly by text, sending her a few pictures of the baby. She texted back to keep the information coming as she was sitting in their hotel room while it rained outside. She joked that there was a fat chance she'd be able to enjoy her vacation knowing what was happening back home. I gave her the information I had—that it looked like K would not leave the hospital with Jessica to live at the maternity home with the caveat that DCFS also chose to send Case home with Jessica under the same circumstances. In fact, Case was born even earlier, also cocaine exposed, and Jessica had left the hospital the next day with her baby in tow. Nothing would surprise me.

The next afternoon, after spending the night and morning with Jessica, I came home again to give her time with the baby alone and to check in with my kids. I spent the afternoon fielding questions by text and decided to post something on Facebook because I couldn't keep up with all of it. Our community had been praying for Jessica for months and had watched our relationship unfold. They had rallied with me to love her in the best ways we could. Without my asking, dozens of people started sending me money via PayPal to help with anything she needed. I included this in my update:

> I am not telling you this because I want you to feel angry about the choices she has made that led her to this moment. She does not need our judgment. I am not telling you this because I want you to feel sorry for her. She does not need our pity.
>
> The Mama who gave birth yesterday to that beautiful baby needs our empathy.
>
> Judgment and pity are the high horse we ride on a low road to disconnecting with our fellow human beings. Empathy is the

rocky, less traveled path to connection and understanding.
Yes, her choices have led to some serious consequences. What we
must consider is the impact that other people's choices have made
on her. She is the one paying the biggest price, and she's largely
paying that price alone.

When I asked for prayer yesterday, Mom being in labor was the very
beginning of what is going to be a long hard couple of weeks for
all of us. It is likely that these days I spend with her will be the best
she's had or will have in the foreseeable future, so I'm going to live
love out loud to the best of my ability.

This is not noble or commendable or noteworthy—it is what we
should strive to do any time we are given the opportunity to help
people in their darkest hours.

I spent that night with her, delivering the gifts my community had
bought for her through their spontaneous giving—several pairs of
pajamas, some loose-fitting clothes for her postpartum body, toiletries,
a soft blanket, some books for the baby, and a suitcase to hold all the
gifts when she left the hospital. I woke up in the middle of the night to
feed K, so Jessica could rest. Checking the time on my phone, I saw a
missed text from my mom from 3 a.m. My Grandma Hazel had died.

CHAPTER SIXTEEN
The Third Sister

On Monday, I went home and waited to hear from our case manager about whether or not K would go to the maternity home with Jessica or to our home. I also spent most of the day trying to stop crying. I was freshly grieving my grandfather's death, and now my grandmother was gone, too. We knew the end was coming for both of them, and I was grateful to have loved and been loved by them for over 37 years. My children had had the privilege of living with great-grandparents, something many never experience. I focused on the gift of their lives to keep myself afloat while we sat with the unknown.

I asked my parents if they could cover school pick up and take care of the girls if I had to return to the hospital to bring K home, and around 3:30 p.m., I got the call. Marcus would meet me there with an investigator to sign paperwork. I called Kelly to tell her I was on my way to the hospital and that K would be safe in our home until they arrived back in Illinois a week later.

Bringing K home was surreal—seeing these three little sisters together was mesmerizing. In that moment, they were two and a half years, seventeen months, and three days old respectively.

All from the same womb. All beautiful. My four kids encircled her and took turns holding her while we snapped pictures to send to Kelly's family. I realize it might sound strange, but taking pictures of the five of them was confirmation that this baby was not ours forever. A sense of peace came over me, and I realized for the first time that this felt different. We were taking care of K because she needed us, but I knew we were making the right decision by giving her to the Meurers long-term.

Later, I would look back at the text messages from Jessica on the day we brought K home from the hospital and weep. She was so defeated and angry. At one point, she told me "congratulations," and I had to fight back the urge to lash out at her. After all I'd said and done to build trust with her, she thought I was over here celebrating? This wasn't a celebration. Separating a child from their mother is never a celebration. With those texts, there was an undercurrent that said she thought I was the one who did this, like I had any kind of control over how this happened, not to mention a complete denial of her part in having her child taken away. Jessica did cocaine shortly before giving birth. That was the reason she didn't take her baby home. She had an open case involving two other children who had already been taken by DCFS. That was another reason.

For over a year, I'd been balancing the stresses of fostering, our military lifestyle, and raising four children. In the last four weeks, I'd moved our family into a new home after a house flood and watched two grandparents die. And then I stood on-call to take a baby whose mother could not care for her while also trying to support that mother. Aside from the obvious grief, I was immensely disappointed because there were many times during Jessica's pregnancy when I believed she was going to make the right choices and reach for something better. When I laid in bed that night, all of this swirled around and embedded deep inside my heart. The result was a quiet rage about how Jessica was trying to spin this as something that was my fault.

At my core, I'm much more a thinker than a feeler. I have spent many years stuffing feelings down or actively trying to out-think them. But this was a moment of reckoning for me. I could not out-think any of this because the weight of my life was crushing. I woke up to get K from her bassinet beside my bed for a feeding. I turned the lamp on, so I could see to change her diaper. She made tiny noises punctuated by sneezes, a side effect of cocaine exposure. While I looked at K, I saw Jessica's face, and it broke me.

Everything that I was experiencing was bearable because in my weakest moments, I could lament to a higher power. In my weakest moments, I could reach out to my husband, my parents, countless friends and other family members, even my boys to give me a minute to rest. I had resources like a home and food and money in the bank to solve daily problems.

Jessica had none of this.

What she did have was broken and abusive relationships, trust and abandonment issues, and unhealthy coping mechanisms. No matter how hard life felt for me in that moment, I would not allow myself to lose perspective. I would feel every single feeling—anger, grief, disappointment, resentment, indignation, disgust. And then I would keep going because the gravity of how we got here was so much greater than this moment that I knew would pass for me.

No woman or girl has six pregnancies by age 21 in a vacuum. No mother wants her baby born exposed to drugs even if she intellectually understands how that happens. Jessica was wrestling with demons far more malevolent than anything I'd ever encountered, and the blame game she was playing where I was the face of everything wrong in her life made sense. It was too great a burden to face personal responsibility in the immediate moments after losing another child. It was too great a fear to acknowledge the people in her life who wounded her. It was too ambiguous a challenge to blame the state of Illinois. So my face, my arms carrying her baby away in a car seat I brought to the hospital, was the best place to direct her anguish. And because I loved her in an inexplicable way, I was willing to take the beating because empathy demanded I share her pain.

CHAPTER SEVENTEEN
The Team

I can't go any further in this story without talking a little bit about our village. I know that metaphor is tired, but it's overused for a reason. As much as it pains me to say this as a textbook introvert, every good and perfect thing in my life is the result of being surrounded by supportive, kind, helpful people. My health and well-being hinge upon striking the right balance between refueling in solitude and depending on others.

From hours after Case arrived at our house, we have had friends and family walking the road with us. Friends and acquaintances dropped off clothes and baby supplies. Others sent meals or gift cards for restaurants. Messages poured in from people I only spend time with online. Being on the receiving end of this kindness has strengthened my resolve to be that kind of friend to other people in need. I'm not exaggerating when I say that I have paused in my day to help someone hundreds of times over the years because there is a tiny voice in the back of my mind that reminds me how life-changing small kindnesses can be. I'm not talking about huge, headline worthy things. I'm talking about answering the phone when I feel like I don't have time, being patient with an unreasonable child, and smiling at a stranger. Even my interactions with Jessica were permeated by the generosity of others. I chose love and grace and peace because that was what hundreds of others poured into me.

My friend, Amanda, grew up with foster siblings, some of whom her parents adopted eventually. When Case came to live with us, she sent a beautiful blanket with Jeremiah 29:11 on it. Two months later, she sent one for Bea. A year later, even knowing that K was not going to be with us permanently, she sent another one.

Veena and I grew up together attending the same private school in Oklahoma City. Because of Facebook, we reconnected as adults, and I enjoyed watching her live as a single woman in NYC. You'd be hard pressed to find someone whose life looked more different than mine the moment we started fostering, but Veena immediately jumped into our life feet first through virtual gift cards. Multiple times throughout this experience, she surprised us with "thinking of you—buy what you need!" gift cards, and they always seemed to come at the right time.

Another childhood friend, Nelson, and his wife, Erin, whom I've never met, sent a mattress via Amazon when I put it out on Facebook that we were looking for a hand-me-down. When a local friend showed up on our porch with one, I told Nelson and Erin that we were mattress rich. They responded immediately to return the mattress to Amazon and use the money for whatever else we needed.

So much is said about the vile world of social media—how it wastes our time and makes us feel bad about ourselves, but that has not been my experience. On some level, I think social media is like anything else—you get back what you put into it. Sure, there are times when bad stuff happens, but just like real life and perhaps even more easily, banishing trolls is up to me. The vast majority of my online interaction with people has satisfied two deep needs of mine. First, I have been able to share our story with a huge number of people who genuinely care about our family. Secondly, I've been able to teach other people about the fostering world, which is so foreign to many and encourage several friends who are wading slowly into the foster waters. Not a day went by that I didn't get a message from at least one person checking in with me to make sure I was okay or to get an update about our case. I learned to create boundaries with my communication because, at times, I had difficulty keeping up with all the love coming our way. What a terrific problem to have.

Ashlie, the friend who showed up on my porch with a hand-me-down mattress, counseled me every time I had legal questions. She read court reports and brainstormed ways forward when I was spinning, trying to figure out if we were navigating the court system as efficiently as possible. Her twin daughters were in Ben's class at school and made it their mission to dress the girls in as many cute puppy shirts as they could find.

My friends, Katie and Tricia, became my sounding boards when I needed to say things out loud that I probably shouldn't have even been thinking. When I think about these two women, I think about that story in the Old Testament when Moses is holding up a staff to help the Israelites prevail in battle. His arms are tired, and Aaron and Hur find him a rock to sit on and then literally hold up his arms. That's who Tricia and Katie were to me, except most often I was sitting in a booth, and they were handing me tacos and/or margaritas.

My in-laws, who all live far away, embraced the girls as their own from day one. Almost overnight, we doubled their gift-giving duties, and no one blinked. From the beginning, they seemed to have an attitude of "this is what we do now." That might seem an odd thing to say, but much like the importance of preparing biological children for fostering, preparing extended family is a priority as well. I have known other families who have not had the same experience as us—friends whose siblings and parents have not been helpful. Sometimes it feels like an active effort to exclude kids in care. Sometimes a reaction feels more like an oversight. Either way, I think lack of support mostly comes from not really knowing how any of this works. Are they supposed to fall in love with your kids in care? They didn't sign up to foster.

The point is—my in-laws, despite the distance, never gave a hint of anything being awkward. They just showed up. They weathered every court date with us, feeling the highs and lows on a weekly basis. They also knew in some kind of innate way when I just didn't have the strength to have another conversation about the uncertain nature of our life.

And then there were my parents, Mimi and Papa.

After living in Oklahoma for most of my life, they made the choice to move to Illinois when we moved to Illinois. They didn't have anything holding them there and were tired of replacing roofs and lawn furniture every few months because of earthquakes, tornadoes, and windstorms. They'd lived in the center of the country during the nine years we'd been stationed on both coasts, and they'd spent those years buying plane tickets to see their grandsons. Before we even arrived in Illinois during the summer of 2014, they bought a house and started scouting the area for all the best restaurants and local adventures. I went from nine years of living far away from everyone with a husband who was gone all the time to a husband who was rarely gone (thanks, desk job!) and two of the world's best helpers.

For two years, we lived our new normal. I was able to start traveling more for my nonprofit work and for writing conferences. I could commit to evening events without having to worry about paying for a sitter. The new normal was totally bizarre. I wasn't responsible for every second of my children's lives for the first time. When Case came to live with us, Mimi and Papa were on vacation in Colorado, but the second they were home, they were at our house running the boys to karate or Cub Scouts or staying with the baby, so I didn't have to drag her out in the cold after bedtime. They were at our house the day Bea arrived, putting together her crib. My mom gave her a bath. My dad rocked her until she fell asleep. Every single step of the way, they have shared in the joy and shouldered the burden of grief with me, and they have not wavered in their support or winced from the pain.

How do you do it? Because I'm not doing it alone.

So in the midst of a dark moment—when I was up all night with a newborn between the deaths of two grandparents—one of my people showed up again. My best friend, Erika, lives in Noble, OK, an eight hour drive from where we lived in Illinois. The day after my grandma died and I brought K home, she texted and said, "I'm coming." I wasn't in a position to say, "This feels like too much." Erika is married with three kids, runs a business, and is in charge of all the things. Seriously, her schedule makes mine look like a cake walk. She's one of my heroes, and I have said many times about her that she is someone who sees a house on fire and runs for a bucket. For her to take time away from her full and important life to sit with me in my grief and fatigue was a tremendous gift.

The night she arrived, we had takeout Italian that our mutual friend, Michele, brought over. Michele is a talented photographer who had taken pictures of Case for free when she arrived. In that moment of crisis for me, Michele was living with the weight of some serious personal crises, yet she showed up with a spread of food love. The next night, Kelly sent money from Hawaii via PayPal and said to buy dinner on their family. On Friday morning, I left all five kids in Erika's care (while Scott attempted to work), so I could drive back to Missouri for my grandma's funeral. I turned around after the graveside service and drove back to Illinois. I needed to be with my mom and her family, and that was possible because Erika and Michele dropped everything and ran to be by my side.

I lived in a constant state of gratitude. Many times since those days when I found myself relying so heavily on my village, I've had this thought: what if the same people who were willing to go the extra mile for foster families were willing to bring that same kind of energy to supporting the families who lost their kids to the system?

CHAPTER EIGHTEEN

The Bridge-Building

Over the next few months, Jessica became more and more distant. On top of the grief and anger she was feeling about losing K, I think she was harboring some resentment because she felt like I had betrayed her by not telling her about Kelly sooner. I struggled with knowing how to navigate that, and it all felt messy. Jessica had a handful of visits with all three girls and was not responsive to my or Kelly's attempts to strengthen our relationship. In the meantime, Kelly and I began getting our kids together regularly—all eight of them. Per the rules, we were encouraged to get the three littles together weekly for sibling visits, but we would have hung out without the rules. At the time, when we were assembled over pastries or sandwiches at my house or hers, our kids were 12, 11, 9, 7, 3, 2, 1, and newborn. It was a circus. And it was fun.

At one point, we invited Jessica to our house to spend time with both of our families. She agreed to come but spent most of the night on her phone and showed little interest in the girls. I was reminded of the time a year earlier when she had been working her service plan and then disappeared for several weeks. I cannot imagine how hard it was for her to walk into our home and look both me and Kelly in the eyes. I cannot imagine how hard it was for her to see our families thriving and happy, while she was cut off from all of her children and embroiled in daily drama with her family. I will not make excuses for her poor choices, but I will always try to understand the underlying issues that caused her to make them.

We knew at this point in the process that Jessica's and Chad's parental rights to Case were going to be terminated. That ball was rolling, and I was determined to treat Jessica with dignity and respect because I wanted the girls to have ties to their family history as they aged. Bea's case was still wide open with a goal to reunify her with her dad, Don. Because of his criminal history and current living situation, I was in a constant state of shock that he was an option but also aware that a judge would decide Bea's fate. We were told again and again that his criminal case had no bearing on his family court case. The more I had time to think about this, the more livid I was with a system designed to not protect children. The majority of the hours I spent in therapy were spent hashing out this particular rage.

My friend, Jamie, runs a coffee shop in Valley Brook, Oklahoma. This tiny town sits on the southeast edge of Oklahoma City and is known for its strip clubs and homeless population. Many of the people experiencing homelessness are dealing with mental illness and substance abuse problems, and some of them are convicted sex offenders who have nowhere else to go after leaving prison. Jamie started the coffee shop in Valley Brook because she recognized that no one likes these people. No one wants these people around. In her book *Beloved Chaos*, Jamie honors these lives with gut-wrenching respect. When she talks about the people she serves who are sex offenders, I listen carefully. Honestly, when Jamie talks about anything, I listen. Period. In a chapter titled "Sex Offenders, Felons, Crazy People, and Transients," Jamie talks about the attacks on her business and family that have happened as the community railed against her efforts to help people who come from hard places. She ends the chapter with a mantra that permeates all of Jamie's writing and life work: "Us *for* them. Us *with* them. Until there is no us or them, only *we*."

At the heart of my concern for Bea's future was a pure and genuine love for a little girl who called me mommy. In the coming months, we would make the decision to separate our family geographically when Scott got orders from the Air Force to change jobs because we were committed to seeing her case to the end. When we asked what we could do to keep our family together, the answer from everyone we asked was "give the girls to another foster home." That was never an option.

When I thought about her returning to a life with her biological father, I thought about safety concerns regarding his past behaviors, but I also thought about the loss she would feel by leaving our family. I thought about the opportunities she would lose in being raised by someone who was aging, in failing health, and had very little stability when it came to his housing. I thought about how hard we had worked to get her healthy—mentally and physically—and how every time she visited him she came home talking about how she didn't like when her biological brothers were mean to her. I thought about how she had di-arrhea for two days after each of these visits. I wasn't sure if it was the McDonald's or anxiety.

In listening to Jamie talk about serving convicted sex offenders in her work and weighing the risk, I decided to reach out to Don. All of my anger and anxiety was not serving me well, and I finally decid-ed that if there was a possibility that we were going to lose our girl, I needed to build a bridge to her father. I needed us to be a *we*. If she went back to him, there was no way we would know what happened to her if we continued being distant and judgmental. If I was going to stay connected to Bea, I had to be Don's friend. For the first time in my life, I truly understood what Jesus meant by loving your enemy.

Bea visited Don every Saturday morning, so my plan was to send him a letter each Saturday with my contact information. I wanted to be available if he was open to communicating. This was my first letter:

Hi, Don!

I wanted to let you know that Scott and I are curious if you would like to meet sometime to talk. We have had the chance to get to know Jessica over the last year, and we regret that we haven't been able to do the same with you.

When Faith came to live with us over a year ago, we had no idea how much we would grow to love her. As you know, she's a bright light. Not only is she beautiful, but she is smart and funny and kind. We are so proud of the young lady she is growing to be before our eyes.

We know that you love her and want the best for her, and so do we. As I said after court the last time we saw you, Scott and I truly believe that she will have the best life if we all view this process as a team. We are with you—on the same team.

I know your time with Faith is limited right now, so we wouldn't want to infringe on your visits unless that is the only time we could meet with you. We would love to take you to dinner sometime, but we also know that your schedule is hectic between work and taking care of the boys. Please let us know if this is something you'd be interested in doing at all, and if you would rather us tag along for a visit or arrange something outside of your visitation schedule. The boys are welcome to join us, of course. We also respect the choice if you decide you don't want to meet with us.

I printed some pictures of Faith for you from the last thirteen months. I hope you enjoy them! Please call or text us if you would like to arrange for a time that we could get together. My cell phone number is XXX, and Scott's cell phone number is XXX. Either of us would be happy to talk. I'm usually easier to find,

*as Scott works in a secure building during the week and
doesn't have his phone with him.*

Hope to hear from you soon!

Always,
Leia and Scott

I wrote these letters for five weeks straight, and for five weeks
straight, there was no response. Our case assistant, Leah, who had been
with us for a good amount of time at this point, confirmed that she had
given him the letters, and I never got a phone call. I was disappointed,
but I also understood that no matter how hard I tried, a relationship with
Don was a long shot. Why would he want to be friends with us? I told
myself each week that I was doing everything I could do, but I would
need to find peace with whatever happened even if the result
was nothing.

I don't really understand how prayer works, and during this time
I felt really disconnected from any kind of higher power. I tried med-
itating on occasion with a prayerful mindset, resulting in the opposite
effect. Alone with my thoughts, I did not feel comforted. If I wanted to
use a super spiritual slant, I could say they were prayers of lament, but
I really just complained a lot. As I wrote these letters each week to Don
detailing what Bea's week had been like, I felt my heart changing. I was
excited to share with him about friends she was making or a new skill
she learned at gymnastics. I sent printed pictures each week with notes
on the back about a day at the park or her new obsession with Peppa
Pig tattoos. Instead of being angry about who Don was or what he did,
I was focused on my girl. Then one day in the middle of that, I started
praying for Don's heart.

For the first time in months, I felt connected to God through prayer.
I felt like I was chatting with a trusted advisor about someone I really

cared about. I prayed for Don's heart to be open to a relationship with us. I prayed for his heart to be protected from the pain of this separation. I prayed for his heart to be healed from past hurts that had nothing to do with any of this. As the days ticked by and we got closer to Scott's departure, there was a desperation to those prayers. But instead of screaming at God because of injustice, I prayed for Don to feel love and accept grace. When other people of faith asked what they could do for me, I started responding each time: please pray for Bea's dad.

The night Don called me for the first time, I saw an Illinois number, and my heart started racing. I'd been sending letters with Bea for five weeks, and he had finally decided now was the time. Before I answered, I had one of those moments when a million thoughts flash through your head. *Is this a courtesy call from a doctor's office with an appointment reminder? Is this a scammy robocall? Is this someone from Boy Scouts calling about camp?* But it wasn't. It was Don.

My heart pounded in my chest when I heard his voice, and I let out a long, slow breath as he spoke. He told me he had read every letter and wanted to call from the very beginning, but he didn't know what to say. He told me he would like to meet with me and Scott sometime, and we decided on breakfast. When we hung up, I burst into tears and in some kind of cosmic moment, Bea came bounding up and hugged my leg. She looked up at me with her big blue eyes and said, "Mommy, why you crying?"

I told her they were happy tears because something good happened.

"Somefing good?" she asked. "I love somefing good."

Facebook: March 26, 2018

Some form of this conversation occurs EVERY SINGLE TIME
I leave the house with the girls:

Other people: Are they twins?

Me: No, they are a year apart.

OP: Oh, that one is older.

Me: Yes, she is 2 1/2, and she is 1 1/2.

OP: They look just like you.

Me: Thank you.

OP: That's a lot of work having two babies so close together.

Me: Yes, it is.

OP: You look great!

Me: Thank you.

OP: Do you have other kids?

Me: Yes, two boys who are 12 and 9.

OP: You don't look old enough to have kids that age.

Me: Thank you.

Not every conversation has each of these elements, but many times,
it's this WHOLE BALL OF AWKWARD. I have given up trying to
tell the truth in any form.

#smalltalkistheworsttalk #fostercare #stopthemadness

CHAPTER NINETEEN
The Breakfast

My friend, Belinda, wrote *Brave Souls*, a book about empathy in which she talks about the horrors of war in faraway places. She talks about how atrocities are happening all around us, and for a lot of people, it's easier to look away. That's not judgment of anyone on her part or mine—I understand why not everyone can look at things like genocide, rape used as a weapon, deaths from preventable diseases, and other horrors and still function in everyday life. In describing her work with women who have been repeatedly raped in war, Belinda struggled to understand how they were able to forgive their perpetrators. She learned from these fierce fighters how they understood that healing themselves could only heal half of their world, that seeing healing in the lives of the men who had violated them was the other half.

Her struggle mirrored my personal struggle with handling my rage and unforgiveness toward Don. Belinda writes:

As I wrestled with the implications of offering empathy toward the perpetrators, I was helped by what's called *empathic dissent*. By not backing away from intellectual and emotional dissonance, it's possible to humanize even those you least understand or most disagree with. Faking empathy has helped me do this. Odd as it sounds, I had to learn fake concern for the perpetrators in Congo. As I asked humanizing questions about the culture that boys grow up in and about why a man would join a militia that promoted rape as a weapon of war, I began to see how Congo's male youth were also victims in many ways.

I didn't have to fake it for long. I learned that some militias force boys to watch their sisters or mothers as they are raped. Sons and brothers are sometimes forced to rape family members. Some boys themselves are victims of rape. As I listened I began to understand the fight many men were making against this culture of impunity, often putting themselves in danger. Many told stories about good men who snapped under the pain and humiliation of a system that uses sexual assault to dehumanize ...

... I broke and began praying human prayers for men who were perpetrators, because so often, they were the first victims. Dietrich Bonhoeffer urged, 'We must learn to regard people less in the light of what they do or omit to do, and more in the light of what they suffer.'

The same goes for foster care. I understand why some people choose to look away from a drug epidemic that is forcing the number of children into care to skyrocket. I understand why some people cannot fully engage in solving the problems of addiction, domestic violence, and child abuse and neglect. But then there are those of us who don't look away, who walk straight into the fire. We can't help it. I don't believe myself to be more noble or evolved than those who can't. Rather, I see my walking into the fire as a way to prove to others that they can, too. So we began building our relationship with Bea's dad. I've heard it said somewhere along the way that it's a lot harder to judge people when you're looking at them face to face.

Our first meal with him was at Golden Corral. He and the boys ate heaping plates of food while we talked about life together. He shared things about his family. He was one of four boys. His mom and stepdad were still alive and living one county over. There were several times that he acknowledged the terrible choices he'd made in his life that led him to this point. I asked him specific questions about what he remembered about the time when Bea came into care. I wanted to know why he hadn't taken her at that point. His version of events didn't match what I had learned from the case managers, and I realized we probably wouldn't ever have a clear understanding about what actually happened.

The boys were on their best behavior. His six-year-old was quiet. His three-year-old sat next to me and wanted me to hold him in my lap. Both Bea and Case called Scott and me "daddy" and "mommy" multiple times throughout the meal. Don flinched a little but didn't comment. When we were done eating, we drove them back to the hotel where they were living. He invited us into his room, and I stepped inside. The walls were wet with condensation. The sheets weren't on the beds. Empty food containers and toys lay strewn across the dressers and the floor. The room was not somewhere I could imagine Bea living even though we'd been told that his living situation met minimal parenting standards. In fact, we'd been told that Bea could return to him while he was living in the hotel as long as he had a crib or mattress for her. He told us that he didn't want that for her. He had plans to get a house. He rehearsed the numbers readily, delineating what he spent every month and what it would take to save up enough for first and last month's rent. He sheepishly told us how much money he spent on cigarettes and pot, adding that he knew he needed to save that money instead.

When Scott talked about his work with the Air Force, Don was riveted. He was fascinated by the fact that Scott flew planes and was an officer. At one point, Don turned to me and commented about how lucky I was to "pull down a flyboy." I laughed uneasily, and Scott responded that he was the one who got the good deal. I asked Don if he would ever be interested in coming to our home for a meal to see where Bea was living and to be somewhere the boys could run and play. He told us he had gotten caught smoking pot on an Air Force base decades before and wasn't allowed to be on base.

The day was cold, and the kids ran around blowing bubbles we'd brought with us. At one point, one of the boys headed toward a staircase, and Don barked at him to come back down. To us, he made some comments that implied the people living on the second story of the hotel were up to all kinds of nefarious deeds. Laughing, he said that DCFS had showed up at his door one day accusing him of allowing his oldest boy to smoke cigarettes. After a good deal of arguing, it turned out they had knocked on the wrong door and were really looking for the twelve-year-old son of the couple one room over. Don added that the neighbors were a bunch of meth heads who fought all hours of the day and night.

When we were ready to leave, Don followed us to the car and helped Bea into her car seat. He kissed her on the forehead and told her he loved her. On the way home, Scott and I talked about how likable Don was. Rough around the edges, but respectful and funny. We were both shocked at the way he owned his "relationship" with Jessica, which had started when she was best friends with his daughter in middle school. He shared that he was grieving the death of his daughter's mother, and Jessica came from a rough family. Each time his story started sounding like an excuse for the years of sexual abuse, he would add something like "I know what I did was wrong." He also said everything he was experiencing now was a result of the bad decisions he made with her. At 54 years of age, he talked openly about the fact that he would prob-ably be dead in the next five years. He smoked and ate fast food every day and had kidney and heart problems. He added that no man in his family had lived past the age of 60.

Scott and I repeated these stories to one another as if we were trying to convince ourselves that the story was real. While I was glad Don was willing to meet with us, I was increasingly concerned about what returning to him could mean for Bea.

One thing foster care has taught me is that we have to live in the moment. Every day was a new normal. Some days were horrible. Some days were beautiful. And there was no way to know what each day would bring. I had to focus fully on what was directly in front of me because hypothesizing about what could be only led to anger and anxiety. I had been told by everyone involved that parental rights cannot be terminated based on what *might* happen. This was perhaps the greatest cause of mental gymnastics for me because I tried to stay grounded in what I knew to be true. Don was not in good health. He was struggling to take care of the basic needs of his two boys. He had a history of sexually abusing a young girl. By all appearances, he wasn't making progress to correct any of these issues beyond attending a basic parenting class that was required by his service plan. Based on what I knew about his efforts and about the way foster care plays out in so many cases, I realized at that time that we could be stuck in limbo for years.

When I said this out loud to Scott, he agreed with me that if this took years, we were in it for the long haul. Scott would move around the country (or world) alone as the Air Force determined. I would live with our four kids in Illinois. Neither of us loved this plan, but there wasn't a single second when we considered anything else. The "system" told us that Bea's relationship with her biological father was worth the additional trauma and instability of a seemingly endless open case. We were literally the only ones directly connected to the case who could fight for her to have a better life.

At the risk of belaboring the point, let me say this: we did not dislike Don. Spending time with him strengthened my belief that as Belinda says, "listening with empathy is a redemptive act." We were all mixed up together in a story of redemption. I felt a sympathy toward him that could only be supernatural. Even knowing what I knew, I understood how the idea of losing Bea forever brought him a tremendous amount of grief, and I listened carefully to his words as he described how conflicted he was. He told us multiple times that day that he knew she belonged with us, that we were her mom and dad, and that we could give her a much better life than he could. He also repeated the fact that he would fight to the end to get her back.

Facebook: June 22, 2018

Conversation with Sister driving her Cozy Coupe car …

Me: Hi, ma'am. What's your name?

Sister says name.

Me: How old are you?

Sister: Two but I be three on my birfday.

Me: When is your birthday?

Sister: August twelve.

Me (as she begins to drive away): Where are you going?

Sister: To August for my birfday.

#fostercare #birfday #celebrate #tgif

CHAPTER TWENTY
The Goodbye

As if the weather was tuned into our plight, spring of 2018 in southern Illinois was uncharacteristically cold and gross. As Jessica's visits continued to be more sporadic, Kelly and I started committing to driving the girls instead of sending them with a case assistant. It was easier for everyone, especially when the visits were canceled or ended early, giving us the chance to check in with Jessica more often as we attempted to include her in our lives. She was working at a restaurant in the mall, so their visits always involved chicken fingers and running around a mostly empty restaurant while a few people played games on the video poker machines.

Our case assistant, Leah, transported Bea to all of her visits on Saturday mornings with Don. Leah quickly became one of Bea's favorite people. She was young and sweet and an anchor in what became increasingly more difficult each week. Bea was moving toward three and starting to understand things more. When people referred to Don as her dad, she would often say things like, "My daddy flies airplanes."

She was too young to really have a conversation about her feelings, but there were plenty of indications that she did not love going to these visits. Being around the boys seemed to bring her stress, as she often mentioned they were not nice. After one visit, I had the same conversation I had with her every time when she returned home.

Me: Did you have a good day?

Bea: Yes.

Me: Who did you see?

Bea: Leah.

Me: Was anyone else there?

Bea: (biological brothers' names)

Me: Anyone else?

Long pause.

Bea: I don't want Don to kiss me.

I sat in shock for a moment because it was such a clear, long sentence. Nothing in me believed that anything bad had happened. I imagined he gave her a kiss when she was leaving the same as I'd seen him do in the past, but for whatever reason, the interaction made her uncomfortable. I told her that was fine, that she doesn't have to kiss anyone she doesn't want to kiss. I made a point to tell Scott and my parents that from now on we should all practice asking her first. For over a year after this conversation, we asked for permission to kiss her, and she often said no to all of us. I shot off an email to Marcus and Leah letting them know what she said and telling them how I handled the issue.

Before another visit, the rest of us were preparing to leave for Ben's baseball practice on a beautiful day. She started crying when I told her that Leah was on her way because she didn't want to leave. She wanted to watch Ben play baseball. I knew she would be fine when she left, and I reassured her that she would love seeing Leah. My positivity in the face of her tears was as much about comforting myself as it was about buoying her tiny spirit.

In April, we attended the first of what should have been three consecutive court dates leading to termination for Case. We were told she would be transferred to an adoption case by June. These court dates became a convoluted comedy of errors as parents didn't show up, the parents' lawyers didn't show up, and the parents got new lawyers. Spoiler alert: Case's termination remained open for another eight months, a total of one entire year from when the judge declared that parental rights would be terminated. In normal people speak, this means that while her parents had no possible chance of retaining rights, the court held her in limbo for a full year because of administrative reasons.

At the end of May, we sent Scott to Oklahoma for some requisite training he needed before moving to Washington. We had a trip planned to meet him halfway-ish in Branson for the fourth of July, and we also planned to spend some time in Oklahoma with friends and family later in the summer about two hours away from where he was training, so we could see him during his time off. We knew we had to be intentional about seeing each other because the last thing we needed was to create more confusion about the big people in the girls' lives. Even as I enrolled all four kids for the next school year, there was a tiny part of me that hoped a miracle would occur at our July permanency hearing.

In June, we had an administrative case review at which we learned nothing new, and the reviewer shared that at this point it looked like the most likely scenario was that Bea would eventually be returned to Don. As I had many times, I pushed for his visits to be longer and more frequent. How was she supposed to go from seeing him two hours a week at McDonald's to living with him? In discussing the form these visits would take, we all understood that the ball was in his court. Everyone involved knew that he needed longer visits that would eventually turn into unsupervised visits and then overnight visits. We were so far from that being a possibility, and Don would have to take some initiative. Even if he didn't, there wasn't enough reason to terminate his rights in the court's eyes. Essentially, he could keep buying her ice cream once a week for the rest of her life if he wanted.

In July we had a standard permanency hearing during which any hope I had of a tiny miracle was dashed. Basically, the judge rehashed everything about Bea's case and then said, "See you in six months."

The girls had not seen Jessica since mid-May, and she had stopped communicating with us altogether. The only thing of real note from that day is that she appeared to be pregnant again.

In August, we showed up for one of a string of court dates regarding Case's termination only to be told to come back next month. I can't even remember why. The delay was possibly caused by one of Jessica's lawyer's personal crises, of which he had many before the judge eventually removed him from the case. Jessica was definitely pregnant and trying to hide her belly beneath a maxi-dress. She had asked for a visit with the girls that was supposed to occur the following day. She wanted to take them to a splash pad, and the forecast was rainy all day long. I attempted to have a conversation with her about the fact that I thought an outdoor activity wasn't a great idea. With our case manager, Marcus, standing next to me I told her I wasn't going to send swimsuits for a visit in the rain, and she needed to come up with a different plan.

She looked me square in the eyes and said, "Fine, be a bitch."

I took a beat and said, "I'm not trying to be a bitch. I just thought taking two toddlers to the park in the rain—"

"You can stop talking," she said, as she stood to leave.

There was no point in trying to reason with her, and of course, the next day, I got the girls ready for the visit, and she didn't show up. Over the next few months, we attempted to schedule visits a few more times before she stopped communicating with Marcus as well.

The kids started school the same week as the disastrous August hearing, and Scott drove away to live in Washington without us.

CHAPTER TWENTY-ONE
The Anxiety

I started noticing a pattern to my emotional landscape. My stress and anxiety seemed less manageable around each court date followed by a letdown when each of those hurdles was jumped. The problem as we moved into the school year was that because Case's termination kept getting moved, I was going to court at least once a month. There wasn't time to recover between each big day. That combined with the fact that Jessica cut off communication and would not confirm whether she was pregnant again almost broke me.

I was juggling our geographical separation from Scott well with my parents' help, and I increased my therapy appointments to weekly. Our schedule felt more regular because Jessica was not requesting visits, and Don was making his visits consistently, so it was easier to prepare for how and when Bea would struggle mentally and physically each week. Kelly became a source of strength for me as she was uniquely positioned to understand what I was feeling. Not only did we share children from the same biological family, but paternity results told us that K was actually Don's, not Chad's. Don said from the beginning that he wanted nothing to do with K because he knew he didn't have the capacity to care for her. Kelly and I metaphorically held hands as I navigated why he was holding on so tightly to Bea, while she navigated why he was denying K.

With every support in place I could think to have, I still felt like I was holding on to the edge of a cliff. In October, I wrote a password-protected piece for my blog to share with our friends and family that speaks to the tension. Here's a segment of what I wrote:

I believe that every single person connected to our case is handling these proceedings with care and caution and following policy and procedure to give Faith's father a fair chance. I believe that every single person involved with our case wants to use common sense within the bounds of the law. I believe that every single person involved with our case understands the gravity with which this little girl's life must be treated. Ultimately, her life is in the hands of a judge whose job it is to uphold the law.

I am trying to be as objective in my telling of the current state of things as possible because my feelings do not matter. It doesn't matter how unjust this feels to me. As a foster parent, I am tasked with caring for the child in my home until she is no longer in my care. I am tasked with advocating for her best interest. That is what I will continue to do.

I am putting this information out into the world because the people who are reading this are the people who are supporting me in my ups and downs. My feelings DO matter to you. Because of this, I need everyone to stop saying things to me like:

Everything happens for a reason.

All of this will happen in God's timing.

God has a plan.

I am going to level with you—while on my good days I have many conversations with God about bringing peace to my heart, about protecting their mother from further harm (she is pregnant and currently using drugs), about softening Faith's dad's heart to understand what is best for her—I spend most of my days shaking my fist WITH God. It is never God's plan for children to be abused. Of course there's a reason for everything—those reasons don't always make sense, and God's timing? Okay.

Please, please, please spare me these meaningless platitudes. My anxiety levels are so high right now that it takes everything I've got to get to the end of the day when I can rest. It is not helpful to try to chalk up broken systems and broken people to God's plan and timing. I also don't need anyone to teach me about free will in a broken world. I've been a Christian my whole life, and I'm well aware of those illustrated talking points.

To say that I'm living in a state of constant lament is the closest I can come to describing life right now. Every time Faith leaves our house, I am devastated. Every time she returns, I do what I can to help her work all of this out in her little, brilliant, developing brain. Let me tell you what it feels like every Saturday when she tells me she wants to stay home with her sister. Let me tell you what it feels like when she tells me, "It's okay, Mommy. I will always come home."

It is the most brutal, raw pain I've ever felt in my life. And we go through it every single weekend. I hold her and read to her and let her throw her fits. I help her every single weekend as she deals with gastrointestinal fallout from these visits. I try to be patient with her

*when she's extra wired or extra grumpy or extra weepy. Because
none of this is her fault.*

*I haven't written in three months because I was hoping to get
a moment when I felt like I could breathe and find perspective.
I was hoping to be able to present some shred of hope, but honestly
I think the best thing I can do right now is to write from the middle
of the storm, so I can look back at this time in our lives and
remember where we've been.*

675 days down.

CHAPTER TWENTY-TWO

The Conversation

Our November court date came in the midst of a flurry of activities typical of that time of year. Having been to court every month since June with the empty promise of Case's parental rights being terminated, I showed up with low expectations.

Both K and Case were on the same termination path at this point, so Jessica and Don and Chad were all technically required to be at court. Chad had never been to a single court date, but Jessica and Don had a good track record of making an appearance.

I knew from her social media that Jessica had spent the last few months traveling with Chad for his job, but it wasn't until I saw her at court that I knew for sure that she was pregnant again. There was no hiding her growing belly.

At this point, all of these monthly court dates blend together in my mind, and I have difficulty remembering which time the case was continued because the lawyer didn't show up or because Jessica didn't show up or because of some other administrative problem, but on this particular blustery November day, we got word from the state's attorney that nothing was going to happen. I stormed down the hallway muttering a string of expletives, practically running to the bathroom to keep from losing it in front of everyone involved.

I threw up in the toilet, the stall door still swinging behind me, and took a minute to breathe while my body fluctuated between hot and cold sweats. I was physically breaking. I just needed to leave. As I walked out to my car, I saw our CASA worker, Mary, walking with Don. I got in the car and tried to calm my nerves. My heart was beating so hard that I could see it pushing against the skin above my left breast. I watched as Mary nodded while Don talked, gesticulating with his hands. I couldn't hear what he was saying, but I imagined he was angry about showing up to court yet again with no progress. Something about his movements encapsulated both anger and defeat, and I thought to myself *same team*. In that moment, I genuinely felt empathetic to his frustrations and realized that my anxiety and his anger were coming from the same emotional space. I rolled down my window and waved both Don and Mary over.

Still visibly shaken, I calmly apologized to Don for my outburst and told him I was tired of showing up to these court dates over and over to have nothing happen. So was he. He was taking days off work for every hearing. Wasted time, lost wages. I told him the thing that set me off was the look in Jessica's eyes when we were all told this wasn't going to be the day. She looked straight at me and smiled like it was funny. I explained that I left to keep from engaging with her in a way that I knew wouldn't be productive.

"Don, I'm going to level with you," I said, looking directly in his eyes. I could sense Mary's eyes on me too, and I was glad she was there to witness the exchange. "I'm not in a great place mentally and emotionally about this. Being separated from Scott and trying to take care of four kids day in and day out is hard enough."

I paused a beat and glanced in Mary's direction. Her face was blank, and she appeared to be holding her breath. I felt like I was right on the edge of a platform deciding whether I had the fortitude to strike out on the tightrope. If I said these things out loud, would my words backfire? Would Don use my emotional state to wound me? Or worse—would he use it against me to cause problems in our case? If I opened up and was truly vulnerable with him, would he see me as human, or would he pour salt on the open wound?

I took a breath and continued. "I know you don't want to be here anymore than I do."

"Hell no!" he said. "I've got to call out from work every time this happens."

"I know you do," I said, hoping to build a bridge through empathy. "I'm sorry. I really am. I need you to know that I'm having a hard time coping with the stress of not knowing what's going to happen. The future is completely wide open, and based on what I know now, it looks like it could be years before Scott can live with us again. You know I'm not a wilting flower. I'm not delicate."

His smile indicated that he knew. He answered, "No, you've— you've proven that you're pretty tough."

"But I need you to know that I'm tired." And this is where I let go completely and started weeping. "I'm really, really tired. And I'm angry. I'm angry because I can't control any of this. I don't do well when things are completely out of my control. You know as well as I do that the lawyers and the judge and this whole process—it's a complete cluster. You know that no one cares about speeding any of this up."

"No, that's for sure," he said.

"So I don't have any power here, and the court has no reason to move forward," I said. "The only person with any kind of power here is you."

He looked surprised, but before he could respond, I kept talking. I had to get all of this out because I had no idea if I would get another chance to talk openly with him face to face. Plus, the ball was rolling, and there was no way to stop it now.

"If you really want her back, you have to start doing more," I said. I wondered what Mary was thinking about me saying this out loud to him. "Do you realize that part of the reason we haven't moved forward is because you've never had her for more than two hours a week? Does that feel like a good effort to get your kid back? Even if by some miracle the court decided at one of these hearings to return her to you—do you think it's fair to her to go from eating ice cream with you once a week to living with you?" I paused for a response. After a few seconds, he said nothing, so I kept talking.

"Don, she has a good life with a routine with people who love her. She is safe and loved and thriving at home and at school. She's with her sister. You know that Scott and I would love to adopt her, but we can't do that just because we want to. Right now, we're being told that the most likely scenario is that this will keep going at the same pace until you do enough to show that you're ready to care for her. When I asked for a reasonable timeline, you know what Marcus said?"

"What?"

"He said there's no way to know, but there are cases like this that he has seen go on for years. YEARS." I wiped my face with my coat sleeve. "We're already two years into this. How many more years do you want to do this? One? Two? Do you want her to live with us for four years and then when she's five years old have her come live with you? Does that seem like the best thing for her? Or for you?"

As my voice rose and my nose began to run, Don crossed his arms and nodded his head a few times. I turned to look for a napkin in the glove compartment.

He started to respond as I blew my nose. "No, that's not right. She shouldn't have to wait that long." And then surprisingly, he had tears in his eyes as he said, "And I'm really sorry about all of this. I'm sorry you're going through this."

I was breathless. This was uncomfortable. I did not know how to feel about his reaction. I'd been angry at this man, had pity for this man, been disgusted by this man. I'd had thoughts about him and his life that were judgmental, hateful, and downright mean. And here he was telling me he was sorry. Every bit of empathy that I'd been pretending became real. While my motives for building a bridge to Don had always come from a pure place of wanting Bea to have her best life, those efforts were wrapped up in my struggle to stop seeing Don as a monster. For the first time, I saw him as human—truly—because his response was so gracious. I was not his enemy, and he wasn't mine. I breathed deeply and said, "Thank you for saying that."

"Well, it's true. Just because I want to get my daughter back doesn't mean I want your life to suck," he said. And then he said the thing he'd said many times before. "I know I can't give her the life I want to right now. Not the life she deserves."

"Okay," I said. "Then what are you going to do about that? Let's talk strategy. I know this sounds weird, Don, but this situation makes us like family. We're raising a little girl together, so even if it feels wrong, hear me out. Let us help you figure this out. What do we need to do to get you to a place where you feel like you can care for her?"

I was just as surprised as he was to hear the words coming out of my mouth. I didn't want her to leave us. I wanted to be her mom for the rest of my life. But at this particular juncture, I felt myself letting go of the illusion or perhaps delusion that I could force any particular story line to play out.

"I'm working on getting a place for me and the boys," Don said.

"Good," I said. "And you'll have a place that's safe for her at this new place?"

"That's the plan," he answered.

"And what about visits? Are you going to increase your hours?" I asked. "I think it's really important that she sees you more often than once a week. And you've got to do something other than buy her ice cream at McDonald's. That doesn't look like parenting. That looks like a fun day out every now and then."

I wondered if I'd crossed a line, but he seemed unphased. "I know. I don't know what else to do with her. The weather's been crappy, so we can't go to the park, and this place we're staying—well, it's not a good place to take her."

I had this fleeting thought—*but it's okay for your boys?* But I let that go and kept plodding through a conversation that was getting easier. "I get that, but you have to figure something out because you're not going to get her back if you don't start working toward unsupervised visits and overnights. That's how this works. And it needs to happen quickly, not a year from now."

"I know," he said. He reached up and rubbed his face. I could feel the tension between us draining, and he looked like a tired old man. "I'll talk to Marcus about increasing my hours."

"Let me know what you figure out," I said. "If we need to coordinate something on a weeknight to get more hours in, I'll make sure she gets there even if there's no case assistant available."

Mary, someone who had steadily observed our case from start to finish and who was tasked with remaining objective as a CASA worker, finally spoke. "I've got to get to another appointment, but keep me in the loop about schedule changes. If I don't see you again, I hope you both have a good holiday season."

And with that, we looked like three friends saying goodbye in a parking garage, wishing each other a Merry Christmas. He thanked me and joked that he'd probably still take her to McDonald's on Saturday, but he would try to extend the visit to four hours.

I drove home and posted a quick update to Facebook asking for space because I didn't have the capacity to interact with anyone about the day. I spent the evening going through the motions of feeding four children and getting them to bed and then fell asleep before 8:00.

Facebook: November 13, 2018

Last week, I had Bea's parent teacher conference, and the report was
as expected—she's happy, helpful, kind, and ready to learn. Today,
I met with Case's teacher, and she told me she wants to work on
helping her "come out of her shell" because she's so shy.

Please join me in this raucous laughter.

#honeybadger

CHAPTER TWENTY-THREE
The Recital

Since her third birthday, Bea had been seeing a counselor every week. They mostly colored and played with stickers and talked occasionally about her feelings. At our administrative review in June, the reviewer had suggested she start sessions in preparation for her transition back into her dad's care. In my mind, the more adults around her who could help her navigate that transition, the better.

I did not want to lose Bea. I believed our home was the best long-term plan for her. Nothing in me believed Don had the capacity to care for her. And yet here I was preparing for that inevitability in the best way I could. She would have her counselor to talk to, and God willing, Don would allow us to still be a part of her life if I kept the lines of communication open.

On the way home from therapy one day, Bea and I had a short conversation that stopped me in my tracks. Under other circumstances, it would have been "normal" or even mundane.

Bea: Mom, what's in your mouth?

Me: Gum.

Bea: I want some gum.

Me: When you are big, you will get to chew gum.

Bea: And I can drive?

Me: Yes, when you are big you will drive.

Bea: And I can wear tall shoes?

Me: If you want to, yes.

Bea: I'll be so happy when I'm big.

In that moment, I was listening to a typical three-year-old who was watching her mother closely. I was the one who chewed gum and drove a car and wore tall shoes. I was the one who was teaching her how to be human in so many ways. The prospect of not seeing these tiny hopes and dreams of hers unfold was crushing. I wanted the assurance that I'd be the one dropping her off every first day of school. I wanted to be the one who talked to her about puberty. I wanted to be the one who drove her to soccer practice and school dances and movies with her friends. I wanted to help her map out her adult life in whatever way she chose. Would she go to college? Would she get married? Would she have children? Would she have a career that took her on adventures?

Even as I wrestled with my anxiety about the future, I knew that our case was not unique. Sometimes foster care stories are shared in a way that makes it seem like decisions are made overnight—that people get the call one day and find out the child they love can be adopted next week, or more often, we hear stories about how a call comes in and the kids go home to their biological parents or some other family member in a surprise gut punch for the foster family.

That happens sometimes. But for a lot of cases—most certainly ours regarding Bea—the process of deciding whether a child returns home or goes to parental termination is an arduous, backbreaking march full of uncertainty, false hope, and devastating blows.

I want people to understand that we (to include our immediate family and all who love her) bore the burden of that uncertainty with as much fortitude available each day because a child's life was quite literally on the line. I'll tell you what this pain did for me. It softened me. It made me more patient. It helped me be a gentler, kinder version of myself because the alternative is to break under the weight. It helped me understand one facet of grief that I'd only witnessed in the lives of friends who walked this road before me, making me more empathetic to their loss.

My conversation with Don in the parking garage had been hard and good. I came home wrecked from the intensity of the court proceedings, but the more time I had to think about my interaction with him, I felt like I'd done the right thing in talking to Don about my concerns.

For all of the pushback I'd experienced from agency workers and the red tape nonsense we'd dealt with on the legal side, it was nearly comical that the only people who seemed to be on the same team at this point were the people who stood to lose the most. If Bea remained with us, Don would experience tremendous loss. If she returned home to him, our family and everyone who had grown to love her would be devastated.

This is a scenario that plays out far too often and is the source of my greatest frustration. If I could wave a magic wand and change something about the way the system operates, I would move cases faster. People within the system have accepted the unacceptable. There are federal statutes that state that if a child has not been reunited within 15 months of adjudication, the state should move forward with termination of parental rights. When I brought this to the attention of DCFS legal, I was told the state courts ruled this statute as unconstitutional.

I am not a lawyer, so I don't know the ins and outs of why this happened, but I can tell you what this ruling means in real life. There are children who age out of the system bouncing around homes and institutions for the entirety of their childhoods. There are children raised for three or four years by foster parents and then returned to homes they've never known. The unnecessary damage we do to kids is disgusting. Maslow teaches us that after physio-logical and basic safety needs are met, human beings need love and belonging most to survive. The way the system holds kids in limbo is a conscious and intentional choice—a complete disregard of what we know to be true about survival and attachment. We have decided that changing the chemistry of children's brains in ways that leave them unnecessarily damaged is okay. The people who make these decisions based on policy and procedure instead of what is actually best for kids have become numb to reality. This numb attitude that has permeated many of the spaces I've entered as a foster parent disregards the humanity of these children.

After talking with Don, I felt like we both understood the most important thing—no one was going to protect Bea but us. If she returned to him, he knew staying connected was important. If she stayed with us, we needed to assure him that we would never cut him out of her life.

During our parking garage conversation, Don had mentioned that he'd left his oldest son with someone that day instead of sending him to school because he didn't have any pants, and the temperature was too cold to go in shorts. He didn't want anyone judging him for sending his kid unprepared for the weather and risk another call to DCFS. In the time I'd known him, he had been hotlined multiple times and cleared of any wrongdoing. He was very smart about not doing anything that even hinted at not meeting minimum parenting standards. I told him I had just gone through Ben's clothes and pulled out all the pants that were too short, and I'd be happy to send them along with Bea at her next visit.

That night, he called to tell me that on his way home from court, he'd stopped by Goodwill to get pants. He also wanted to apologize again for upsetting me in the parking garage. I told him it wasn't his fault that I got upset and that talking with him actually helped alleviate my stress. I told him I'd still send the pants on Saturday. Before I hung up, I paused to think about how I wanted to handle something that I'd not said in the parking garage. My heart pounding, I blurted out a question before I could stop myself from asking. "Bea has a ballet recital next month. Do you and the boys want to come?"

It took him a few seconds to respond, but when he did, he sounded excited. I gave him the details about the time, location, and the cost of tickets. I almost offered to pay for his tickets but then decided to leave that to him. I also told him that he needed to be aware that Kelly's family would be there as well. He had maintained up to this point no interest in having any connection to K for a variety of reasons, so it was only fair that he knew she might be there.

The day of the recital, Kelly and I both arrived early to get our dancers backstage and stood in the lobby waiting for everyone else to arrive. She decided to leave the baby at home with a sitter to keep things simple. That morning, Don had called to tell me that he was bringing the boys, a young girl who lived upstairs in the same house as them, and his mother. I'd never met his mom before and from what he had said, I was expecting someone quite elderly. Instead, Kelly and I looked out the window and saw Don with three kids and a beautiful, elegantly dressed woman. She carried herself with poise and was cordial if a bit reserved when we first shook hands.

Bea was part of two dances, and we giggled uncontrollably as she stood eyes wide, staring at the audience without moving her feet a single time during either of the dances. On the inside I hoped she would at some point realize she was on stage and follow the steps her teacher was doing just behind the curtain, but she could not get over the lights and sounds. I turned to my mom and whispered, "At least she's not crying." I wondered if Don and his family were feeling proud of her as she bravely stood in her tutu or if they were feeling nervous or awkward about being together at this event.

At the end of the recital, we agreed on a place to have lunch and headed to our cars. On the way to lunch, I rehearsed in my mind the things I would say to Don's mom. How much did she know about us? What did she know about Don's current standing with his criminal case? Did she know about K?

When we sat down to eat, my questions sort of melted away as Don's mom steered the conversation. Before we could even order, she turned to me and said, "I have been telling him from the beginning that he has no business raising that little girl. He needs to surrender his rights and let you adopt her."

I looked down the table at Don, unsure if he heard over the sounds of trying to get the boys settled in their seats. I turned to her and said, "I appreciate you saying that. We would love to adopt both of the girls and keep them together."

Without much prompting, she went on to state that it was obvious that they were well cared for and loved. I knew Don could hear her when she said a few disparaging things about how she wasn't sure how Don turned out the way he did. At one point, he interjected and said with an uncomfortable laugh, "I'm the black sheep."

Everything about this exchange felt like an underwater dream. In the moment, I was both cold and sweaty. I felt a sense of pride at the way she recognized how much we loved the girls. I felt oddly protective of Don when she talked about all the mistakes he'd made in life. Eventually, the conversation turned more to her life. She told me about her house and her husband who was dealing with health problems. She told me about her three other children and her other grandchildren. In the meantime, Don made conversation with my parents at the other end of the table. I offered to pay for the meal since they came by my invitation. Don's mom insisted on giving me some cash to cover their portion. I left the girls with my parents, so I could pull the car around because the afternoon was unusually cold. When I came back, they had obviously been deep in conversation. Don's eyes were full of tears, and he thanked me for inviting them to the recital.

Later, as we went about our Saturday, my mom and dad told me that he told them he knew the right thing to do was to surrender his rights. He knew allowing the adoption was the best thing for her. He knew he could not give her the kind of life we could. He knew she was exactly where she needed to be. My mom told me that his tears came when Don told them that he just didn't want Bea to think he didn't want her.

I saw a glimmer of hope in their eyes, and a small part of me thought that maybe this conversation really was significant, a real turning point in our relationship with Don. But most of me was too cynical to believe this conversation meant anything. I'd been having these same conversations for a long time, and I couldn't count the number of times he had said similar things to me with the caveat that he would never be able to give her up—that the state would have to force his hand. I wished that he had not talked to my parents like this because it was crushing to think about the trauma they would experience when we lost her. Like many times before, I felt the burden of trying to protect everyone else from the pain. Intellectually, I understood that my parents were responsible for their own feelings and reactions, but that didn't stop me from wanting to shield them from the ups and downs. I would suffer with false hope, but they shouldn't have to.

I knew that her life was in Don's hands because I had no power to persuade anyone to move faster, and the state had no legal reason to terminate his rights. He was the one who got to decide whether Bea continued to be a ward of the state while our family was geographically separated indefinitely. Her life, our lives, depended on him.

Facebook: December 7, 2018
What I said: Eat your lunch.
What Sister heard: Eat your lunch at Olympic record speed, so you can have one Starburst.
What Baby heard: Walk around shirtless and shoeless with a backpack and a doll saying "Baby go poop!" over and over with a comically concerned face. Stop to eat some chalk. Beg for a bubble beard from the kitchen sink dishes. Avoid eating at all costs.
#toddlermom #tgif

CHAPTER TWENTY-FOUR
The Other Perspective

By December, Scott had officially been living away from us for seven months. He was preparing to take command of the 57th Weapons School Squadron at McChord Field in Tacoma. The change of command was scheduled for December 19th, so the kids and I flew to Washington for the ceremony during winter break. Scott's parents, sister, aunt, and a close family friend flew in from Oklahoma City, Chicago, and Dallas.

When Scott and I were in premarital counseling, we came up with some short-term and long-term plans for ourselves as individuals and as a couple. At the time, Scott's longest term career goal was to be a squadron commander. His biggest dream felt like light years in the future to two kids fresh out of college, and here we were gathering with our family and friends to watch his dream play out in real life. Before the ceremony, he and I stood at the back of the banquet hall joking about how we weren't really sure what was supposed to happen next now that he peaked.

We spent those few days surrounding the change of command hanging out with our friends and family who had gathered and being tourists in the town where Scott was living without us. He had been renting a room from a family, so we met them briefly and helped Scott organize his belongings—most of which fit in his Civic—as he prepared to move into a new place after the New Year. Somehow in a week's span I was celebrating my husband's biggest accomplishment while he was living like a college kid.

The stars aligned during our trip, and we housesat for some friends because they were out of town during the exact dates of our stay. Until we flew back to Illinois, we caught up with friends we'd made the first time we'd been stationed at McChord, attended Christmas Eve service at our home church, and opened presents Christmas morning around someone else's tree.

In my memory, Scott and I didn't have a single conversation about the case. Anything that we would have said out loud would have put a damper on our holiday cheer. In some unspoken way, we'd agreed to enjoy every bit of our time together without talking about the stress of the unknown. On January 2nd, my parents, the kids, and I boarded the plane back to St. Louis and drove home to our base house on the other side of the Mississippi River while Scott moved his carload of things into a basement studio apartment that belonged to the father of one of our friends. I joked that I'd give anything to live by myself in the middle of the woods for a week, and Scott laughed, but I regretted it as soon as I spoke because I knew how painful this entire situation was. As hard as it was for me to navigate the daily drama of foster care, Scott's struggle was in feeling like he couldn't do anything to alleviate the pain. I had the comfort of knowing my efforts were advancing the cause, and Scott felt sidelined and in the dark. Later, I asked him to tell me what this time was like for him, and he wrote this response:

On the morning of August 28, 2018 I sent my family out the door for school like I might on any other work day, only this day was different. My work that Tuesday morning was driving from

Scott AFB, Illinois to a new assignment at Joint Base Lewis-
McChord, Washington ... alone. Before beginning my journey I
figured I should run back into our house to make sure I hadn't left
anything out while packing the night before. While inside check-
ing all of my usual spots, I stopped to hug our dog and weep
(Bokonon has always been solid when I needed a good cry).

After passing awkwardly by one of our neighbors with a face full
of tears, I hopped in the car and set out on my three-day journey.
All things considered, the trip was rather enjoyable as I stopped
to visit close family friends at three different points along the way.
As I left my last friendly stopover, however, the enjoyment came
to a screeching halt. Those last two hours and some-odd minutes
between Portland, Oregon and Olympia, Washington were filled
with a sinking feeling like I had rocks in my belly.

This feeling came from the fact that I was about to accomplish the
one career goal I've ever really had in the Air Force—to serve as
a Squadron Commander; but I was facing the reality that I was do-
ing it while living 2,168 miles away from my family. Many officers
who deploy to take command are away for 12 or 13 months, but
the time horizon is set before they leave; there is a date they can
target when they know they'll be back with their families. I had no
such date, and I was "choosing" to live away from my family at
a stateside location.

This reality hit me squarely in the face as I pulled up to the house
where I was going to live for the next ... year? Two years? All three?
I did my best to shake off the emotion and walked up the steps to
meet five complete strangers who were also my new roommates:
an elderly family patriarch, his daughter, great-granddaughter,
and two grandsons, who had agreed to let me rent a room.

They were all very welcoming and offered me a seat at the kitch-
en table where they had finished brunch a little while ago. The
patriarch insisted I eat, so I chose a cold waffle as I wasn't about
to ask him to cook a new one, and he decided to pair it with a can
of Country Time lemonade. So there I sat, drinking my lemonade
and eating my cold waffle on a paper plate with a plastic knife
and fork (the patriarch was a bachelor who swore off dishes
in his later years).

At the end of "brunch," the patriarch handed me a piece of mail
from my wife, and I did my best not to completely lose it in front
of him. After barely making it through the door to my room, I sat
down with the card and opened it to reveal the new SIM card for
my phone. To say it was not the most romantic card is an under-
statement, but you'd never have guessed it by the time I spent
reading it.

The next morning I went to work, where I knew I would find refuge
and a place to compartmentalize all of the uncertainty and grief.
I would leave early for work and stay late at the base to work out,
only arriving home with enough time to shower, eat, and head to
bed. Some nights I would depart a little early to grab a beer with
friends who knew what our family was going through.

Each quarter I would sit with our schedulers and block time to
fly back to the Midwest for long weekends and family vacations.
I would also sign up for every trip away from Washington as I could,
as there was little point living in a house with anyone other than
my wife and kids. I would wait for each new court date, hoping and
praying that Leia would call with news that would provide clarity
into our future, but each time seemed to bring another can kicked
down the road.

Exhaustion is probably the only way to describe my state of mental preparedness as I entered Squadron Command. I didn't know when I would live with my family next, and I was about to undertake an immense professional task.

Life in the military provides its share of uncertainty; I've deployed six times and been extended on deployments and shorter trips alike. Despite that experience, nothing compares to the uncertainty and frustration of living in the foster care system; I used quotation marks when I said "choose" earlier because our foster care workers advised us to turn the girls over to another family when I received orders to Washington. We chose love and stability for them over staying together as a family. We dedicated time to our foster daughters and their biological parents alike ... it was one of the most rewarding experiences I've ever been a part of, but the path we walked was filled with uncertainty, loneliness, and emotional exhaustion.

CHAPTER TWENTY-FIVE
The Surprise

On a Friday afternoon in the middle of January, I cursed the weather as I tried to run errands. The high was something like 32°F, and we needed groceries. Running around with two toddlers who were still recovering from being off schedule for all of winter break did not scream TGIF, but it was life.

My phone rang as I pulled into the Walmart parking lot, a notorious dead spot for my cell phone coverage. It was Marcus, and he asked if I had a minute to chat. Most of our communication happened via email. Phone calls usually involved bad news—court was canceled, visits were canceled, extra visits were happening, or I was required to jump through another pointless hoop because someone had lost paperwork along the way.

I stayed in the warmth of the car with a tentative connection as he asked if I would be available for a family team meeting on Monday. Family team meetings were always on the table but had to be initiated by bio family, so we'd never had one. Ideally, these meetings could happen regularly and be beneficial to everyone. I remember during training thinking how participating in conversation with the whole team was the best way to move kids through the system efficiently. Communication was key. What a naive thought.

Scrolling through my mental calendar, I checked off how I could get the girls' child care covered and fit a meeting into my day and told him that I would, of course, love to meet with Jessica. She had requested Kelly be there as well. At this point, Kelly and I discussed Jessica's well being regularly. We knew she had to be at least at the end of her second trimester. We knew from her social media that she was spending a lot of time with Chad traveling. She wasn't talking to either of us, though, so we were worried. Was she healthy? Was she going to doctor's appointments? Was she using?

After discussing the Monday meeting, Marcus mentioned that the weather was supposed to be bad during Bea's regular visit with Don Saturday morning. I'd told him that if Leah was unable to transport Bea because of weather, I'd be willing to facilitate a visit on Sunday if the snow cleared up. Marcus told me he would let Don know the plan.

I hung up with Marcus, loaded the girls into a cart that was parked near our car, and rushed into the store, the cold air biting my cheeks. I'd barely made it to the produce area when my phone rang again. I knew it would be Kelly. Marcus told me he was calling her next, so I anticipated an unpacking session. Strolling through the cereal aisle, I opened a package of breakfast cookies to give to the girls while Kelly and I discussed what this meeting could mean.

"Why do you think she wants to meet with us all of a sudden?" Kelly asked.

"I mean, she knows her rights are being terminated for Case and K, so she probably wants to talk about Bea," I answered.

"Why does she want me there then?" Kelly asked.

"I don't know," I said. And I really didn't. "I guess even though she intellectually understands what's happening, until this is officially done, she's always going to hold out hope that she's getting her kids back despite the fact that she's done nothing to make that happen. Maybe she wants to talk to us about the new baby?"

"Do you think she's going to ask us to take this one?"

"I think she's going to try whatever she can to keep this baby honestly."

"Do you think she even can?" Kelly asked. "She's going to get flagged as soon as she walks in the doors of the hospital. There's no way they'll let her keep this baby!"

The difference between me and Kelly at this point was that I had a year more experience with the nonsense. Many of our conversations went like this—Kelly stating what felt like the obvious, me reminding her that we should never assume anything. One of the things that bonds me and Kelly, not just as foster-in-laws but also as friends, is that we both operate from a space of righteous indignation. We both have big feelings, big reactions, big motivations to fight what we view as injustice. At this stage of the game, Kelly was far less jaded than me, so her perspective—this statement that surely the system would do the right thing for this new baby—grounded me and kept me from diving deep into the negative.

"From what I can tell, I don't think she's making great choices, but we really don't know," I said. "Whatever she wants to talk about, Monday will give us a way to check in with her and see how we can support her."

We hung up after I told her I needed to get through the store before the girls lost their patience. I finished shopping, grabbed the boys from school, and drove home through a flurry of snowflakes. That night, we ordered pizza like we did every Friday night. I texted Leah about the bad weather and then sent a text to Don as well: "The weather looks bad for tomorrow. Hopefully Marcus told you that I am willing to make something work on Sunday if it clears up. Stay warm and safe!"

Snow fell consistently all night and most of Saturday. First thing Sunday morning, I got a text from Don that said, "Don't look like the roads are going to be safe, maybe later today it might be clear who knows. I can come to O'Fallon but it's not looking good, give her a hug and kiss for me and tell her I love her and miss her so much."

The timing of the Monday meeting was the day before both a termination hearing and our next scheduled permanency hearing. We would meet with Jessica on Monday, and then we'd all go to court on Tuesday. We had two time slots for court. That morning, we'd go to our eighth hearing in ten months to terminate all parental rights for Case. K's case had been added to Case's when her legal screen passed in August, so Kelly would be there hoping for the same end to this ridiculous ride.

Later that afternoon, we would come back to discuss Bea's permanency plan. I anticipated the judge kicking her case down the road six more months because Don had complied with his service plan and had increased his hours with her. The only wild card was a psychosexual risk assessment he'd been required to take. Don talked openly about his annoyance at having to do it but also told us that he would do whatever the state asked to get Bea back. He'd undergone hours of testing, and the case manager was waiting on the results of the test. Everyone hoped the results would be back in time for the permanency hearing. If the results came back that Don was unlikely to offend again, it could work in his favor in moving forward faster. If the results came back that he was likely to offend again, it could potentially be the reason the judge would not place her back in his home.

Monday morning, I dropped the boys at school and then took the girls to my parents' house, so I could head to the agency office for our family team meeting. Kelly and I had discussed how we really wanted Jessica to control the conversation. We wanted her to have the space to lead us where she needed to go. She took the initiative to have this meeting, and this felt significant, even if we weren't sure what she wanted.

Jessica, Kelly, Marcus, and I gathered around a table, and Marcus said there was a possibility that Don was going to call in if he could step out of work for a few minutes, so he laid his phone on the table.

Marcus had talked to Jessica about how going back and forth to court about the termination wasn't good for anyone. He had talked to her about surrendering her rights instead of waiting for the termination process to play out. She started slowly, but she stated very clearly her intent for the meeting. She and Don had been talking over the weekend about the court hearings.

Jessica wasn't mentioning an undercurrent I knew was in play. Over the past three months, Don had told me many times that if he surrendered his rights and Jessica somehow got Bea back, he wouldn't be able to live with himself. That was the final reason he wasn't surrendering, even though he knew it would be best for Bea. He wanted to make sure Bea was safe with us.

Listening to Jessica speak about surrendering her rights to Case and K made me feel proud of her. She understood that the state was going to terminate her rights, and this was one way of taking her power back. I am completely aware of the paradox here. Giving up her parental rights was the only way she could control her own narrative. She understood how powerless she was, but she also understood that surrendering meant she played an active role in building a better life for her children. On a very basic level, she was giving them—and us, their foster parents—the gift of her consent. She was choosing a better life for her kids even if the decision meant enduring the excruciating pain of a permanent loss.

At some point in the conversation, she shifted to talking about all three girls, and I realized something I suspected but hadn't allowed my brain to process. She was discussing surrendering her rights to Bea—the child whose name she tattooed on her arm, the child with whom she had the strongest bond of the three because she had spent more time with her before the state took her away. No legal screen had been filed for Bea because of Don's consistent involvement, so surrendering rights to Bea held a different weight completely.

At least from a legal standpoint, the door was still open for Bea eventually being returned to Jessica's home. Over the course of the last two years, she had on several occasions discussed how she knew that if Don could get Bea back, she would move back in with him and get to be an active part of Bea's life. The victim's protection order from his criminal case regarding their involvement during Jessica's childhood would eventually be lifted, and she knew they would no longer risk getting in legal trouble for spending time together. Don, of course, maintained that he would never allow her to move back in. He knew they were bad for each other, and he was concerned about the way she interacted with their boys as well.

But now she was talking like she was considering surrendering her rights to Bea too, and it sounded as if this was because Don had convinced her that this was the best plan of action. She talked about how she didn't want to take Bea away from Case. She talked about how proud she was of Bea, how smart she was, how she loved knowing that Bea got to do things like gymnastics and ballet. I listened to her talk, and this moment was the most confident I'd ever seen her.

After a few minutes of discussing how she might surrender all rights at court the next day, she got to the heart of why she called the meeting. She looked mostly at me when she talked, glancing occasionally in Kelly's direction. "I know we haven't been talking a lot. And I know the last time we was in court, you got really mad."

I smiled and nodded yes. I didn't want to interrupt her.

She continued. "I don't know if you're mad at me and if you would just ... like stop talking to me or whatever if you have the girls, and I would want to know what's happening to them or whatever and see them if I could."

It was such a telling moment, her trauma laid bare in the most vulnerable way. This was a girl—a woman now—who had sacrificed so many times for the sake of others only to be left hurt and alone. I had tried my best to build a cocoon of trust around all of us, to show her how much we loved her, to lead her to understanding of safety and stability, and in the end, she still didn't really trust me.

I had that feeling in my chest like an elephant was stepping on my rib cage, like my heart was sinking into my gut, and I answered the only way I knew how. "Jessica, I know it doesn't make sense, and I don't know if you even believe me, but I love you. We all do. Our whole family loves you, and I'm sorry that I didn't reach out more since the last time I saw you. I'm not mad at you. I'm mad at this whole situation. When I got mad at court, I should have said I was sorry."

I didn't say anything about how one of the reasons I hadn't reached out was because I didn't know if she had a working phone number. I didn't say that I felt like she owed me an apology. Looking in her eyes, I felt ashamed and ridiculous about feeling like she owed me anything at all.

I said, "Whatever you decide tomorrow will not change how I interact with you moving forward. I will still love you. I still want you to have a good life. I want your baby to be healthy and loved. Everything I've promised you before is still true—I will do my best to make this awkward situation less awkward. I'm committed to keeping our relationship open. That hasn't changed even if we've had a couple of bumps in the road. There is nothing you could ever do to make me mad enough to cut you out of our life."

She was crying. And listening.

"I can't promise you that everything will be perfect or that I won't make mistakes, but I can promise you that I will always try my best to fix it when I do make mistakes," I looked over at Kelly, and I felt strengthened by the look in her eyes. "I love your girls, Jessica. I think you know that and believe me when I say that. I know you have no reason to trust me too. But please know that if you decide to surrender your rights, I will never cut you off. I know you haven't known Kelly as long, but I can promise you that she feels the same way."

They shared a moment in which Kelly reinforced this idea. I ended by adding, "I want you to also know that as far as anything bad that has happened between us over the last year, I've already forgiven you. I don't want there to be any kind of bad blood between us. I hope you'll forgive me for all the times I fell short of loving you the way you deserve."

That night, I tried to fill Scott in over the phone about how the meeting went, but there was no way to adequately capture the feeling in that room. There was no way to convey the significance of every single detail. And there was no way to explain why the overwhelming feeling I had going to bed that night was dread. Being a foster parent for the last two years had been a master class in crushing disappointment, every lesson the same theme. I'd learned to guard myself against feeling any sense of hope or joy in an effort to cushion the inevitable blows.

For much of our case, I'd shared publicly through my blog important milestones. I processed many of the ups and downs with a wider audience in the beginning because our cheerleaders wanted to know everything—the victories and the defeats, the moments of faith and of doubt. Over time, I started limiting my sharing with a handful of family members and friends until eventually, I stopped sharing because the whiplash was too much to process with more than one person. Because Scott lived in another state, I often processed with Kelly or my mom, and then eventually, I had to protect my mom from the pain as well. It was hard enough carrying my own emotional trauma. Psychologically, I couldn't afford to carry the weight of others' trauma as well. By this point in the case, I was basically radio silent on social media, sending the occasional "we have court today" text to a handful of loved ones, and in an act of self-preservation and a desire to shield Scott from carrying a burden with no way to be actively engaged, I kept everything inside until I sat down on my therapist's couch.

My mom and I dropped all four kids at school on Tuesday morning, the day after this meeting with Jessica, grabbed coffee at a little shop on Main Street, and headed to the courthouse. Like so many times before, we sat in the hallway with dozens of other people waiting for their turns. Don made a point to sit by me and asked how the meeting the day before went. He mentioned he wasn't able to step out of work to join by phone, but he was hoping Jessica told us about their conversation over the weekend. When Jessica arrived, Don took her to a corner out of ear shot to talk. While they were talking, Marcus told Kelly, my mom, and me that the risk assessment results came back. He couldn't tell us what they were, but he would have to testify to them at the permanency hearing that afternoon.

Marcus joined Don in the corner to talk to him about the risk assessment, and Jessica sat near us. She was quiet and teary eyed. All of the corner whispers felt dramatic, and we busied ourselves chatting about where we might grab lunch between hearings. Our CASA worker, Mary, talked about what she'd done that weekend with her grandkids, and we all talked with other people in the hallway with whom we'd become acquaintances after seeing each other in these hallways month after month. One older couple was caring for their two grandchildren and seeking termination of parental rights as they were losing their son and daughter-in-law to heroin. Two foster moms who shared brothers from the same family were meeting for the first time. One bio mom was feeding her baby and hoping this was the day the judge told her she got to take him home for good while his foster mom chatted quietly with a case manager a few seats away.

Amid the murmured conversations, I looked up to see Don standing in front of me. Jessica stood next to him. With tears in his eyes, Don said to Marcus, "We're ready. Where do we go?"

Marcus stumbled a bit over his words and asked, "You're ready to sign surrender paperwork?"

"Yes," Don answered. "Go ahead and get all of them ready."

"All of them?" Marcus asked. "Do you mean you want to sign for both girls?"

"Yes."

Marcus looked at Jessica, "And you want to sign all three?"

She nodded, letting him know she was ready. Marcus looked through his bag once and then told everyone he had to run to the office to get the paperwork for Faith because he was only anticipating the surrender for the younger two siblings. He did not think Don was going to surrender for Faith today. Our case could be called any minute, so he said that if we got called in to tell them about the new development and that he would be back as soon as possible.

As Marcus rushed off to get paperwork, I stood and embraced Don as he wept. I could see from the corner of my eye that Kelly was hugging Jessica. I stepped back, and Don continued to choke back tears before saying, "It's right. It's what we need to do."

Not two minutes after Marcus left, the assistant state's attorney walked out of the courtroom and asked where Marcus was. Don and Jessica had moved down the hallway, so I told her they were waiting to sign surrenders on all three girls.

Her eyes widened, and she said, "All three? Faith, too?"

"Yes," I said. "I know. We were all surprised."

She stepped back in the courtroom for a minute and then came back out and informed us that if Don and Jessica followed through with signing surrenders, we could finish all business during the morning hearing because there would be no reason to come back for a permanency hearing.

Marcus came back and took Don and Jessica into a meeting room for what felt like hours. When they emerged, he handed a stack of paperwork to the bailiff who was standing at the courtroom door. I avoided making eye contact with anyone and tried to keep my face blank. I held my breath like an Olympic swimmer.

We were in front of the judge long enough to have our names on the record and for him to read the official verbiage related to surrender. He briefly spoke to Don and Jessica to confirm they understood what they were agreeing to, and then the final signatures were taken.

Two years, one month, two weeks, and two days of tension was released in three minutes.

CHAPTER TWENTY-SIX

The Doctor's Appointment

I don't think anyone knew how to feel leaving court on Tuesday. In a matter of moments and with the stroke of a pen, we went from thinking Bea's case might be open for several more years to finding out all three girls' cases would be closed in the coming months. Now it was just a matter of paperwork.

Seeing the girls' first parents' signatures next to the judge's signature should have been reason to celebrate, but the truth is I had two separate breath-stopping feelings as we walked out of the courtroom. First, my brain said, "They say this is the end, but I don't trust it." Next, I held back vomit, a ball of tension settling in my throat, as I looked at Don and Jessica. My friend and fellow adoptive mom, Jody Landers, famously said: "A child born to another woman calls me mommy. The magnitude of that tragedy and the depth of that privilege are not lost on me." In the immediate moments after the surrender, I wanted to cry for all this meant for the parents who created and birthed my children.

My children—nothing felt truer than this phrase, but equally true is that these babies were their children, too. I've read books and asked questions of my adopted friends and talked with experts about how to handle the conversations that come later in life, and I land in the same place over and over again. The truth matters to everyone. When in doubt, tell the truth. Part of our truth (and this may not be the case for other adoptive families) is that I knew before we were ever given the option of adoption and throughout the case and beyond that I wanted to leave the door open for connection to the girls' past. Since the first day I heard the quotation in Mr. Hartman's eighth grade U.S. history class, I loved what Faulkner said about this: the past isn't dead. It isn't even past. And the truth is that Jessica and Don and Chad and Scott and I are all their parents.

The reality is however we choose to frame the stories we tell the girls about how they joined our family. Their first family is not the distant past. Their first family is made up of living, breathing humans. Their first family members know the answers to questions that I don't. Their first family members love them even if they can't care for them. As the girls' second and forever mom, it's my job to control the narrative and to create healthy boundaries until they are old enough to regulate for themselves in the same way I do for the two children who joined our family by birth. We are making a conscious, intentional choice to include the girls' first family in our lives in whatever ways they feel comfortable. I made that promise to them before the adoption, and I meant it.

I've heard the concerns from many people about how leaving the door open to the girls' first family might be confusing for them. Yes, it might, and when they come to me with their questions, their sadness, and their anger, I'll sit right in the middle of the pain with them and tell them the truth. We cannot predict the future, but we can prepare the best way we know how.

After the surrender, there was a visible change in Jessica's demeanor. She seemed lighter, and she was certainly more open. What I've learned in navigating this awkward, unpredictable relationship is that we share a sliding scale of grief and relief. On what was sure to be one of the worst days of Jessica's life, she told me and Kelly that she needed a ride to her doctor's appointment in a week. She was supposed to have an ultrasound to get a better idea of her due date because she hadn't seen a doctor since the first appointment confirming she was pregnant again.

If this seems bizarre, it's because it is, but Kelly and I agreed to accompany her to her appointment. The conversation was short and simple, covering the logistics of who would pick her up and what time we needed to be there, and then we moved forward as if this monumental thing hadn't just happened moments before.

As we left the courthouse, I invited Jessica to Bea's eye doctor appointment on Friday. Even though I'd told her countless times that I had no intention of cutting her off from the girls, I didn't know if she really believed me. I knew—because she had told me the day before in our meeting with Marcus—that her biggest fear was that if she surrendered her rights, she would never hear from me again. I was determined to calm her fears in an immediate way, and inviting her to go to the doctor's appointment with us felt like a necessary olive branch in building her confidence that I would follow through on my promise.

The night before the appointment, she texted asking if it was okay for her mom, Melissa, to come with us, too. I agreed. At this stage, the girls had not seen Jessica in eight months. The times they'd seen her before she stopped asking for visits were erratic and not pleasant for anyone involved, so I wasn't sure how they would react to having her in the car.

On the way to pick up Jessica and Melissa, I told the girls that we were going to take some people to the doctor's appointment with us. I didn't want to say "your mom" because that concept would not have made sense to them, but I also didn't want to say "Jessica." I thought it best to guide as needed in the moment, so I stressed to them the same way I would on any excursion with friends that we all needed to be on our best behavior and use our manners.

When we pulled into the driveway at Jessica's parents' trailer, she and Melissa were already standing outside waiting for us. Melissa climbed into the front seat and asked me if she smelled okay, adding that she didn't want to smell like smoke around the girls. Jessica climbed in the back next to the girls in their car seats. Everyone was smiling, and Bea used her manners by saying, "Nice to meet you. What's your name?"

I heard Jessica laugh uncomfortably, and I am a little ashamed to admit I acted like I hadn't heard Bea's question. My arm pits were immediately wet with cold sweat as a million thoughts went through my mind. Melissa said, "What'd she say?"

And Jessica repeated Bea's words, "She said 'nice to meet you, what's your name?'" before turning to Bea and saying, "I'm your mom. You don't remember me?"

I stared ahead at the highway and held my breath. I met Bea's eyes in the rearview mirror for a second, and then she looked away. I don't know what her three-year-old brain was doing in that moment. I decided to at least acknowledge the situation, so I said to Jessica, "She's so little, and she hasn't seen you in eight months. It will probably take her a little while to remember."

The rest of the day was ... normal? I don't know. I'm well aware that none of this feels normal, but for us, awkward was our new way of life. Jessica and Melissa played with the girls in the waiting room. They took some pictures and joked about how terrible they looked. They asked questions about how the girls were doing in school. Bea saw the eye doctor, and Jessica asked the doctor questions as well.

After the appointment, we went to IHOP because everyone was hungry. We ate together. Jessica took Bea to the bathroom at one point, and I had a quick conversation with Melissa about how she thought Jessica was doing. Melissa was concerned about Jessica not seeing the doctor enough during this pregnancy. She was concerned about Jessica hanging out with a guy who wasn't any good for her. She worried that if Jessica wasn't careful, she'd lose this baby, too.

Over the last two years, I'd learned the very worst things about the woman sitting across the table from me. I didn't want to like her or love her. In fact, looking at her and thinking about how her mothering or lack thereof was one of the greatest contributing factors to Jessica's traumatic childhood made me want to hate her. But in that moment, as she talked through mouthfuls of pancake, she was a mom worried about her baby. Again, I was reminded how hard it is to judge and hate people when you sit face to face.

Facebook: January 25, 2019
A Portrait of My Friday Morning …
Baby: I want pickle!
Sister: Mommy, I love you.
Preteen: Here are seven time-sensitive things I forgot to tell you.
Teenager: I was thinking about how The Outsiders highlights the disparity among socioeconomic classes, and even though the book is more than fifty years old, it's relevant today.
Me: Coffee.
#tgif #momlife #bestlife

CHAPTER TWENTY-SEVEN
The Hospital

The same day that we went to Bea's eye appointment, Marcus called and said that the maternity home where Jessica lived during her pregnancy with K was willing to take her back. We were all shocked at this news because Jessica's last stay at the home had ended poorly. The director said she was willing to give Jessica a second chance, and Kelly and I committed to helping get her settled.

The next Tuesday, we moved her back into the facility and accompanied Jessica to her doctor's appointment where we all discovered she was much further along in her pregnancy than she thought. It was the last week in January, and the new baby was due mid-March. The ultrasound technician confirmed that she was having another girl.

Now that the fate of our three girls was relatively settled, we knew Jessica needed us more than ever. She promised that she wasn't using, and urine tests reflected that truth. Kelly and I talked to her about how moving into the home and staying clean would increase her chances of keeping this new baby. We knew she would be flagged at the hospital no matter what, but if we were going to help her break the vicious cycle she was in, we had to put supports in place that would allow her to find a greater purpose for her life. At the home, she would receive counseling, live with other women in similar situations, and have resources like transportation and childcare.

Over the next month, Kelly and I took turns making sure she made it to her doctor's appointments. We communicated regularly with the staff of the maternity home, so we were all on the same page about moving Jessica toward responsibility and independence. We used our best judgment to help in ways that empowered her and trusted the experts when they told us to help in ways that didn't enable Jessica to fall back into negative patterns. Overall, she was the healthiest by far that she had been since I met her two years earlier.

Facebook: March 27, 2019
Fact 1: the girls love going through the car wash. Fact 2: we have conversations every day about living with Daddy soon. Result: the baby yelled, "I want go car Washington!"
#thisistwo #vocabulary

The girls and I regularly picked her up to take her to lunch. A couple of times, we went to the public library to play and check out books. We helped her get her first library card. She was hoping to enroll in GED classes and needed to improve her reading skills. She applied for jobs, and we drove her to the trainings. When she quit her jobs, we encouraged her to not get anxious about working. She made good choices. She made choices that disappointed us. She showed signs of feeling hopeful about bonding with her baby and staying clean. She felt like nothing she tried would ever be good enough. And Kelly and I kept showing up to feel all of these pressures with her.

On February 27th, almost two weeks before her due date, my phone rang at 4:00 in the morning. I answered, and it was Kelly.

I also had a text from Melissa saying Jessica was headed to the hospital. Kelly and I arrived disheveled in our middle-of-the-night glory and sat on the couch in Jessica's hospital room. Her labor had been strong, but once she was in the hospital bed, it stalled. This was a woman who was well aware of what labor felt like, and she was frustrated. We told her to get up and walk around, but she was tired. Finally, after about twelve hours of monitoring, the doctor sent her home because she wasn't dilating. We told her to call us if something changed and went on our way.

Around 8:00 that evening—about four hours after we left the hospital, I got a text from Melissa that said, "Jessica's phone is dying baby is here" I called her, and she filled me in saying that Jessica had returned to the maternity home, and active labor started back up within minutes. She walked around the kitchen with everyone there telling her she needed to go back to the hospital. Later, she would tell us that she didn't text because she didn't want to be embarrassed if it was another false alarm, and we all came back to the hospital for nothing. She called a friend who said she'd take her to the hospital. By the time her friend arrived, they barely had enough time to get to the hospital room. Twelve minutes after they walked through the doors, Baby S was born.

Kelly and I were there half an hour later. Over the next couple of days, we learned that both mom and baby tested negative for drugs in their system, and Jessica held her breath while she waited to see if the investigator would allow her to take S to the maternity home. In the end, S was released to Kelly's care until some paperwork could be processed. Kelly chose to bring Jessica into her home as well. Jessica was allowed to be with her baby as long as Kelly was supervising. Once the paperwork was processed, Jessica and S were allowed to return to the maternity home together.

I marveled at the difference a year made in Jessica's life. I'd been here before when K was born, and I vehemently argued that Jessica had no business taking K home. This time around I didn't think we were wrapping up this story with a Hallmark happy ending, but I believed enough in Jessica to argue that she should be given a chance to care for her child. In a full circle moment, the investigator who had allowed her to take Case home two and a half years earlier was the same investigator who allowed her to take S home. The difference was Jessica was now surrounded by people willing to fight for her to make a better life.

CHAPTER TWENTY-EIGHT

The Next Right Thing

When Don left court after surrendering his rights on that cold day in January, I honestly had no idea if I would ever hear from him again. In our last interaction, he didn't seem angry. He seemed defeated. In our conversations in person and in text, he sang the same refrain: I know this is the best choice for my daughter, but this is the hardest thing I've ever done. My response was always something along the lines of "I know, and I'm sorry, and I promise to never cut you out of her life."

On that last day in court, I told him, "I know you don't have any reason to trust me, but if there is one thing that is true about me, it is that I always do what I say I'm going to do. This doesn't make sense, but you need to know that we love you and want the best for you. We are connected for life whether we like it or not. Because you are Bea's first dad, you're part of our extended family. Thank you for giving her—and us—this gift."

We cried together, and I meant every single word with my whole heart.

Scott had a trip home to visit us scheduled for mid-February. During a phone conversation I asked him if he would be willing to meet up with Don. I thought getting together with Don and the boys would be better with both of us there. Even though Scott's visit was a few short days, he agreed.

All of this was uncharted territory—what was this relationship supposed to look like? What did healthy boundaries look like for the adults involved? What did healthy boundaries look like for Bea? What kinds of conversations would we need to be having with her to help her understand this unconventional dynamic as she inched closer to being four years old and having a better understanding?

We adopted the theory of doing the next right thing in the choices we made. The next right thing was always whatever honored humanity. The next right thing was always driven by love and grace. The next right thing didn't always feel like the easiest thing, but it was always the thing that brought us peace.

We met Don and the boys at a Cracker Barrel near where they were living at the time. He'd moved them into a basement in the house of a woman who was also providing childcare for the boys while he was at work—a huge step up from the hotel they'd been living in previously. We shared a meal and said our goodbyes with hugs all around. I told him to let me know when he wanted to meet again.

Over the next couple of months, I heard through the grapevine that things had gone south with his rental situation. He was relying on his daughter a lot to care for his boys, and he was sleeping in his van, all of their earthly possessions piled in the back. He went radio silent, and I knew in my gut his silence meant he didn't want us to know what was happening. Almost three months passed before I got a text* from him in the middle of May.

Don: *Hello Leia and Scott and family, want to start by saying how much the boys and I really miss Faith,*

---

* I edited Don's texts slightly for readability, but the content is still the same.

it's like a piece of me has left. I never knew how much
impact it would have on my boys. They ask about her
and ask me why I gave her away. I don't ever answer
them because it's hard giving a answer to young kids
that won't understand anyway, but one thing
I lay my head down every night knowing she is in
a better life than I could give. It would be nice if
the boys could somehow spend a little more time
with her, so I reckon what I'm asking is if anyway
possibly sometime soon can boys see her again.
Thanks for everything.

Me: *Hi, Don! Sorry it took me a minute to get back to you.*
I was cleaning up dinner and taking care of S.
I'm watching her until Jessica gets off work.

I would love to get the kids together sometime or
meet with you if you have time. This is the last week
of school, and our schedule is crazy all week, and
then Scott's mom and sister are visiting for Memorial
Day. Could we plan for something after Memorial Day?

I would be happy to meet at a park or restaurant
sometime. I know you're at work a lot, so let me
know when would work best for you.

Don: *Anytime after Memorial would be fine. Scott*
and you have a lot tougher schedule than me. Let me
know what works for you guys and I would love to
see Faith again.

The next day the conversation continued.

Me: *I missed your call because I was picking up Jessica and the baby to take them to daycare and work. Call me on your lunch break.*

Don: *Damn you adopted more than two kids it sounds to me. LOL*

He called later that afternoon, and we set up a time when Scott was in town to visit him and the boys in their new trailer. They were living about forty minutes from our house, so Scott and I put on a movie in the car for the girls and headed north. We had a couple of boxes of clothes, household goods, and food that we'd gathered as a housewarming gift. In a month, the kids and I would watch the moving van pull away with our stuff headed to Washington, so I was in that purge mode that happens before every move. That same weekend while Scott was home with us, we contacted a real estate agent in Olympia to walk us through a house on FaceTime and put in an offer. The owners accepted our offer pretty quickly, so we loaded some smaller furniture into the van with us after consulting Don about whether or not he would be able to use any of the items in his new place. He told us he'd take anything we had because they were starting over with nothing.

When we arrived in the trailer park, Don was sitting on his porch smoking a cigarette and watching his boys ride their bikes. He immediately hopped up and walked to Bea's side of the car to get her out of her car seat. I carried Case inside, while Don carried Bea, and Scott started unloading the tables and chairs from the back of our van. Inside the trailer, a couple was standing in the kitchen talking.

"Leia, this is Tammy and Cam," Don said, motioning to them with his free hand while holding Bea up with his other arm. "This is …"

He looked over at me, searching for the right way to explain our dynamic. I smiled and reached out to shake his neighbors' hands. "I'm Leia. My husband, Scott, is bringing in some things."

Cam shook my hand and headed outside to bring in the furniture and boxes. Tammy was tall—maybe over six feet, but she couldn't have weighed more than 110 pounds. She had the skin and sunken eyes of a meth user. She smiled, showing huge gaps in her teeth, yellowed and rotting. A boy probably eight years old or so came bounding into the trailer and wrapped his arms around her waist.

Tammy put her hand on his back and said, "This is Jaden."

Don spoke up. "My boys and Mason are thick as thieves. That's how we all met. I'm paying Cam to help me paint and fix the place up, and Tammy has been keeping us fed. Only problem is we only have a couple of pots between us, so we have to keep going back and forth from their place to mine to eat depending on where she's cooking."

Everyone laughed in that easy way friends do, and Don added, "We're making it work."

I was struck by the sense of community I felt in that moment. Cam and Scott carried in two chairs we'd had in our living room that we couldn't use in the new house in Washington. The kids ran up and down the hall between the living room and the bedrooms in the back. Tammy and I unloaded the food we'd brought into the fridge and freezer. Amid the activity, Don stared at me wide-eyed. "What on earth is all of this?"

"I told you I was bringing you a housewarming gift," I answered over my shoulder while putting homemade soup from my mom in the freezer. "It's really perfect timing. I've got to go through all this stuff before the move, and there's no way we'll make it through all this frozen food in the next month."

"Leia, this is too much," Don said.

"No, it's not," I answered. "It's actually really helpful to me and is forcing me to go through our stuff to decide what we can use in our new house and what we don't want to move with us."

I wheeled the cooler out of the kitchen into the living room about the time the guys were putting the furniture in place. Don joked, "Man, it almost looks like someone lives here!"

The furniture was crammed together a little in the center of the room because they were still in the middle of painting, but when all was said and done, Don and the boys would have a nice sitting area with two chairs, a side table, a coffee table, and a TV with a small entertainment stand. Will and Ben even sent one of their game systems instead of selling it back to GameStop. Don remarked that his boys would be excited because they'd never had any video games before.

"Give it a minute, and I bet you'll love it too," I said before explaining to him how the remotes worked and shuffling through some of the games to point out which ones might be best for the boys' ages.

"I'll have to have someone explain it all to me," he said. "My old brain doesn't get all this new technology."

"I bet the boys will have it figured out in no time," I said. "Kids have a way of knowing this stuff innately."

"Maybe this will keep them from begging to play on my phone all the time," Don said.

The whole time we'd been talking, Bea and Case were standing close while the boys ran in and out of the house. I leaned down asking Bea if she wanted to go play, and she shook her head no. Case found Scott and raised her arms for him to pick her up. When he did, Bea moved toward him saying, "Daddy, I want to hold you."

He picked her up, too, balancing the girls in each arm. If Don was bothered by Bea calling Scott "Daddy," he didn't react. Before we left, Don showed us the rest of the trailer, and I asked him point blank if there was anything urgent we could help him with.

"I've bombed the place twice for roaches, and it's getting better," he said. "But a bed for the boys would be nice, so we can get their mattresses up off the floor. They've been sleeping at my daughter's house because we don't got any sheets, and I've been sleeping in the car. Don't bother me. I'm used to it, and I can't sleep in here the nights after I bomb the place."

I told him I'd look online and let him know if I found anything. I'd seen lots of beds and frames in the past on Facebook Marketplace,

VarageSale, and other buy/sell sites. I told him at the very least I'd make sure the boys had a bunk bed. He assured me that I didn't need to do that.

"I know," I said. "But I want to."

We decided to take the kids to lunch at an Italian restaurant in town. We told Don to order whatever they wanted because lunch was on us, and he got teary-eyed. "Look, you guys have done too much," he said for about the fifth time that day. "I appreciate you, but you really don't have to do this."

I paused to think about how I wanted to respond. Don was in his mid-fifties, raising two boys, and struggling every single day to live. He was in poor health. He had strained relationships with his family members. He was living in a place that was better than a car or a hotel but that, in his words, was "no place to raise these kids." He was realistic about his situation, and he wanted better.

I started slowly and felt a supernatural peace about the words coming out of my mouth. "We know we don't have to do this, but we want you to know that we are here for you. We know how hard the last couple of years have been for you, and I hope you understand what I mean when I say I'm proud of you for finding this place and getting on your feet."

"Thank you," he said quietly, looking down. I hoped he didn't feel pitied because that wasn't my intent, but I'd also had enough conversations with him to know how deeply wounded his pride was. "My plan is to live here for a year or so and then find something better. That place is full of meth heads, coming up asking me for money or trying to sell to me all day and night. I'm glad the kids can ride their bikes up and down, but I can't leave them outside alone."

"But it's a step in the right direction," I said.

"Yep—and as soon as the state quits taking half my paycheck for child support, I'll have a lot more wiggle room to get some of my debts paid off," he said. "When I've got that extra money, we'll be fine."

One of the consequences of the adoption was that once the paper-work was finalized, Don's wages would no longer be garnished. The amount taken out of his paycheck really did approach half of his pay.

"I like hearing that you have a plan," I said. "I think that's really important to keep thinking about the future and about making a better life for your boys."

"You know I've been seeing the counselor the last few months," he said. I didn't know this, but I was glad to hear it. "And I'm going to get C in there too to help with his anger issues. He's got a lot of stuff inside him he needs to get out."

I watched as his two boys wrestled in the booth beside him, pausing in their play to take bites of bread and spaghetti. Don popped C on the top of the head telling him to calm down or he'd have to take him outside.

I smiled at them and said, "They're fine."

Don said, "No, they need to use their manners in a restaurant. This ain't McDonald's."

As we wrapped up lunch and headed to the parking lot, I remembered something I left in the car. Running to get it, I heard Don asking Scott questions about being a pilot. The last thing I heard before I was out of earshot was "I bet you're happy to have everybody back with you."

I pulled open the passenger door and took out a framed picture from the last time we'd seen Don and the boys. They were gathered together with Bea in front of the restaurant, bundled in winter coats. I handed the photo to Don and said, "I thought you'd like to have this. It will make your new place a little prettier."

"Damn, she's beautiful," he said, staring intently at the picture and then squeezing his eyes together. He shook his head a little as if this motion would shake the tears away. "Look at me being a damn cry baby."

Over the next few weeks, I shared with our community about how much progress Don was making and how proud of him we were.

The reaction from our people was one of uncomfortable healing for all of us. While I had guarded many of the details about our case from the "public," many people knew about Don's criminal behavior. This part of our story always elicited the most visceral reactions—no one wants to be friends with a pedophile. No one wants to empathize with a pedophile. No one wants to believe that a pedophile is anything but a pedophile. These are not judgment statements. If I rely on my own strength and understanding, I live in a seat of unforgiveness for the lasting damage Don inflicted on Jessica. This is a human response. I don't fault people for having strong feelings about this.

However, as we shared about Don and the boys with our family and friends, we as a community began to pray for space to open in our hearts to love them. One late night, I got a text from one of my family members that said, "I pray for him and the boys every day. I hate to admit this, but it took me a while to pray for him. I know that sounds horrible. I always prayed he would do the right thing for Bea, but I just never prayed for him. I say this a lot but I am thankful for this continuous story that I get to have a front row seat to and be a part of in a small way. It teaches me so much."

She sent this honest text right after she bought several items off of a housewarming Amazon wish list I'd put together for him. I did this at the request of our village—they were all at different stages of working through their complicated feelings about our situation, but they still wanted to help him and the boys get settled in their new place. We bought bunk beds and bedding, everything they needed for the kitchen, cleaning supplies and toiletries, underwear and socks, board games for the kids, and a mattress for Don. He told me the day after we delivered everything that it was the first time he'd slept on an actual bed in over two years after sleeping on hotel floors, in a tent, and in his car. He called out that day at work to paint his trailer, and he said he was going to crawl back in bed for a minute to enjoy it. By our estimation, about 35 people bought something off of that Amazon wishlist, and I like to think that every single one of those people was trusting us to do the next right thing even though it was hard.

Facebook: May 30, 2019

Recording last night's events for perpetuity:

Will: Mom! I think Case took the Chloraseptic from my room.

Me: Where is she?

Case: I right here!

We find her standing in the hallway. She smells medicinal, and her hands are stained.

Will: What did you do with the bottle?

Case: I no know.

Will: You smell disgusting. Where is it?

Case: I no know.

Will: Case. Where is the Chloraseptic bottle?

Case: I no know.

Will: YOU DO KNOW. YOU ARE LITERALLY RED-HANDED.

And then I found the empty bottle in the guest bedroom in what can only be described as a murder scene—splatter all over the floor and walls.

Me: I found it!

Case: Oh no. What happen?

WE LOVE HER SO MUCH. One day her curiosity is going to cure a rare disease or uncover some great archaeological find. Until then, my Spotbot gets used daily.

#thisistwo #everyday #honeybadger

CHAPTER TWENTY-NINE
The Adoption

Our adoption date was scheduled, and I started planning a little party. Several of our friends and relatives were making arrangements to join us, and for the first time I felt like I wasn't trying to tread water with ankle weights. Forever was going to be a reality. And if this was a Lifetime movie, this is the part where an upbeat song would start playing as we walked into the sunset with our four practically perfect children.

But in the immortal words of the Avett Brothers, "I don't want to be in love like the movies/Cause in the movies they're not in love at all/With a twinkle in their eyes/They're just saying their lines/So we can't be in love like the movies." There was no script provided for what happened next, no After the Final Rose to bring back all the characters for a rousing, entertaining reunion.

We wouldn't be able to tie a giant red bow on our life and yell "That's a wrap!" Because in real life, adopting a child or children doesn't suddenly make everything that got us to this point go away. And because we had committed to loving our girls *and* their parents, Jessica was still very much a part of our life. She was living with her new baby in our town. We were seeing her weekly and helping with the baby when we could. During one of our visits, she asked if the Baby K's adoption was going to be the same day as ours. She had seen my announcement on Instagram. I told her we weren't sure when their adoption would be. And then she said quietly, looking away from me out the car window, "Kelly said I could come to their adoption if I wanted to."

I let a beat pass and then said, "Do you want to come to ours?"

"Yes."

"Okay, you can," I answered. "I wasn't sure if you would want to come, but we would be happy to have you there." Those were the words that came out of my mouth, and they were mostly true. There was something beautiful about her wanting to be there and us wanting to include her, but there was also a split second where I thought to myself, *"Can't I have this one thing just for me?"* And then I also thought, *"Why would she want to put herself through that?"*

I have always been a bit of a klutz in the kitchen. When I was pregnant with Will, I was draining a pot of hot water into the sink and lost my grip. The water splashed up and scalded me through my maternity shirt. I yanked it off as fast as I could and started spraying my belly with the sink sprayer. Within seconds the burn was red and bubbling. I had burned myself before on a curling iron or after being out in the sun a little too long, but this was different. When I delivered Will, I still had gauze covering a patch of skin about three inches long and two inches high. The nurses had to work around the area to make sure the monitor didn't rub.

To this day, it's the worst burn I've ever personally experienced, and the wound was healed about three weeks later. Over the course of those weeks, the pain decreased daily as the blood and ooze became less severe. At times, I covered the wound with antibiotic ointment and bandages. Other days I left the bandages off to let it dry out. Eventually, the wound was an ashy scab, then a discolored patch of skin, and then something most people would never notice unless I pointed it out.

I thought of this one day when I was thinking about Jessica coming to court with us for the adoption and what I knew about her life before we knew her. She'd been burned by her family, burned by the men from whom she sought love and acceptance, and burned by herself. When we met her, she was a girl on fire.

Our friend Jim started a nonprofit to get solar lights into the hands of people living in abject poverty in West Africa. Because of energy scarcity, people use kerosene lamps to light their homes at night, which is not only dangerous because of the black smoke they inhale, but is also a common reason people are tragically wounded or die. During a trip to Sierra Leone, Jim met a little boy named Sorie, whose body was covered in third degree burns from a kerosene accident. Because he had no access to medical care, the skin between his chin and chest had grown back in a way that hindered his ability to shut his mouth. Jim and some other friends were able to get Sorie to medical professionals who improved his life dramatically through surgery. Later, The Sorie Project was started as a way to empower entrepreneurs in Sierra Leone, Ghana, and Togo to be able to start solar light businesses, so that families like Sorie's have a better alternative to dangerous kerosene.

The fire we'd watched Jessica walk through over the last two and a half years left the emotional equivalent of Sorie's third-degree burns. Unlike a second-degree burn like the one on my belly when I was pregnant, a third-degree burn leaves serious scars and can take years to heal. Third-degree burns can cause infection, blood loss, shock, and death. In many cases, they don't even hurt because nerve endings are damaged. The fastest way to heal a third-degree burn is through a skin graft where injured skin is replaced with healthy skin from somewhere else on the body. What I was astounded to learn is that when this kind of surgery is successful, the new skin starts developing blood vessels within 36 hours. The damaged area accepts new life almost immediately.

At this point in our journey, it felt like we were helping Jessica with her skin grafts. Allowing her access to our adoption hearing felt like surgery. She would still have scars. She would still be in recovery for a long while. But it felt like a step toward getting blood flow to the places she most needed it.

In the end, Jessica did not come to the hearing for reasons she didn't share with me. The transition from foster family to adoptive family is sticky for everyone. We're all trying to figure out what works and what hurts. Before we packed up to leave Illinois, there were days she wanted to spend time with the girls. Other days she felt hurt and angry that they didn't call her "mom." She texted sporadically asking about how they were and then went silent for a week or so. I stopped by to give her some clothes for her baby one night while she was with her parents. They asked me if I was willing to text pictures of the girls occasionally. Jessica told them, "She does when I ask. Also, I can see them on Instagram anytime I want." This was an answer to their question but also felt like she was stating out loud what boundaries felt good to her.

On adoption day, we were surrounded by family and friends. The entire proceeding took less than five minutes. After two and a half years of sitting in the hallway of the courthouse dozens of times for hours at a time, the actual adoption felt unreal. We walked in, answered a few questions, and took some pictures. If that sounds anticlimactic, that's because it was. Afterwards, we asked the boys what they felt, and Will said the thing we were all thinking: "I mean, they've been ours for a long time, so this doesn't feel any different."

CHAPTER THIRTY
The End

I've struggled with knowing where this book ends because it's certainly not the end of the story. As soon as I think I've found the right place, something important happens, and I feel like it needs to be added. Suffice it to say—fiction has the freedom to end. Stories like these do not. As long as I am alive to type, I will want to add a new paragraph, a new lesson learned, a new reminder of how fragile life is, a new moment in time when any number of the people involved in this telling succeed or complicate things or become their own heroes.

Our last week in Illinois was spent over tearful dinners and play dates and stop-by-for-a-hugs with the friends we had grown to love during our five-year stay at Scott Air Force Base. We were staying in an AirBnB in Mascoutah, a town near the base, and Kelly and I organized an effort to help a woman who was fostering her seven nieces. A couple of Facebook posts and phone calls to key people resulted in coordinated pick-ups and drop-offs of furniture, cleaning supplies, clothing, toys, and other essentials. Aunt Sheila, as we began to call our new friend, was grateful for the help, and coming alongside someone who was willing to give so sacrificially for the sake of these seven children felt like the perfect way to end our time in Illinois.

Amid the goodbyes and the shuffling busyness of helping Aunt Sheila, I knew I would need to intentionally connect with Jessica for a last meeting before we moved thousands of miles away. Everyone involved seemed unsure about how to proceed. I knew in my heart that I was trying my best to distract myself with activity, so I didn't have to feel all the big feelings about our move, especially in regard to what this meant for our relationship with the girls' biological family members. Jessica and I had had a couple of text exchanges about in-person conversations about what "normal" was going to look like when the adoption was official and when we didn't live in Illinois anymore. I tried my best to support her in wrestling with what that meant for her, but I also knew that I wasn't necessarily the person with whom she would want to process all of those emotions.

For the two weeks before we moved, I wasn't sure which was the best number to reach her because her phone was not turned on. She was checking in sporadically from a text app when she could connect to WiFi, and the texts would often come through with different phone numbers attached to them. At one point, she asked when she could see the girls again, and we agreed to meet on Monday morning before we flew to Washington Tuesday evening. I texted her mom, Melissa, to confirm because I wasn't sure which number was best to reach Jessica, and we were meeting at Melissa's house where Jessica and S were living.

When the girls and I arrived, Jessica's parents were waiting in the front yard with S. The girls hopped out of the car, excited to see the baby. Jessica's dad, Buddy, scooped up Bea, who is always more apt to warm to people, while Case held tight to me for the first few minutes. Melissa told me, with a mixture of anger and embarrassment on her face, that Jessica had left the night before to spend the night at Chad's house, and Jessica didn't have a ride back to their house.

Jessica wasn't there. She would not see the girls "one last time."

Frankly, the girls didn't know the difference. They were happy to see the baby and to play with toys in the yard. Both Buddy and

Melissa took turns holding the girls in lawn chairs while we caught up on how things were going for them. Melissa had been working at a fast food restaurant that was walking distance from their trailer park, but the hours of standing were wreaking havoc on her feet and the new management had messed up her paycheck and were acting like they weren't going to pay her, so she was looking for a different job. Between selling plasma and Buddy's disability checks, they were making ends meet. Their younger daughter was still working at a grocery store, a job she loved and that paid well. They helped watch her son when they could.

Melissa asked a lot of questions about our move: would the girls be in school? What was Scott's new job? Were we excited about living in Washington? Did we think we'd be back in Illinois anytime soon?

By all appearances, we were neighbors in the front yard passing the time while we passed three babies around and took pictures. We talked a little about Jessica, but I tried to steer the conversation other places so none of us were trampled by the elephant in the room. I hated that Jessica didn't show up because of what it meant for her—she didn't get to say goodbye, but I also understood that her not being there was either a conscious or subconscious form of self-preservation.

I cannot point to any other relationship in my life more complicated than my relationship with Jessica. I feel fiercely protective of her. I have been disappointed by her many times in the same way I am when my children make poor choices. I am heartbroken for her when I connect to her on a motherhood level—I will never understand the pain of losing a living child. At the same time, I am confident that adopting the girls was not only the best thing for them, but also the best thing for her, as she was not equipped to care for them.

In the weeks after we moved to Washington, Melissa texted me regularly asking if I had any new pictures of the girls. Occasionally, I'd send a picture unprompted if we were doing something special. Melissa and I settled into a good rhythm of communicating. At one point, a good friend asked me if keeping that line of communication open was taxing on me emotionally. While I understand the root of the question, I feel like texting the occasional picture to Melissa is the smallest kindness I can offer. A text costs me virtually nothing emotionally or otherwise. On the flip side, she reminds me every time how much she misses the girls and how much she loves them. About half of her texts also involve some reflection of how grateful she is that they have such a good life. She is experiencing loss, too. There is no amount of texts that will fill the void, but I hope my willingness to keep the door open makes the pain less acute.

About three months after we settled into our new house, Jessica started texting again gradually. She and S were living with Chad. She was clean. She was staying in contact with Kelly, going to church with her occasionally. We bonded over conversations about how hard it is to care for a baby. Between Thanksgiving and Christmas, she texted to let me know she was pregnant again. I tried as best I could to talk to her about her options rationally. I could feel her frustration—she knew this was not good for her body, and she was nervous about adding another baby to their household when taking care of S was already so challenging. For the first time, I felt like she had a true understanding of her decision-making agency. She was considering adoption, and without my bringing it up, after the ultrasound that told her she was having another girl, she told me she wanted to get her tubes tied.

Here are the things I think about often. We love Jessica. We want her to succeed. She's smart and capable and good at setting goals. I've never known anyone who can keep dates and times straight in her head like she can. When she's motivated and hanging out with people who lift her up, Jessica talks about having a job, a car, and her own place to live. All of those goals are attainable as long as she stays clean and focused. She deserves a good life. At once, we have high hopes for her potential but also understand the reality of what it will take for her to reach her goals. I hope she knows she is loved and worthy.

In the meantime, we've continued following the call of the Air Force, moving wherever they send us. After taking a break, we reopened our foster license. Not long after we found out that we would be able to adopt the girls, I was in the car with the boys, and I asked them about their feelings regarding foster care in general. Will had never wavered about his opinion that we should only ever have four kids in our family. I, however, had an unspoken desire to still be involved in foster care in some way in the future even after the girls were adopted.

Will surprised me with his answer as he easily said, "I don't think we should adopt any more kids, but I would be open to having more kids if they were with us temporarily."

What was shocking to me was that despite the emotional toll so much of this had caused—the living in limbo, our family geographically separated from Scott—Will was willing to stay open to the pain of the unknown. Ben said he agreed. The thing that most people fear most about fostering, the idea that we could pour our love into the life of someone or someones knowing we would someday say goodbye, was not a pain too great for our family to bear.

I know these things are true: we are, all of us, stronger than we might believe; we can never exhaust the depth of love it's possible to give and receive; and we are trying our best.

EPILOGUE

Our family uses the term "first parents" to describe the girls' biological parents. This is a phrase we chose to reflect our feelings about adoption. Our adopting the girls does not erase the fact that they had parents before they met us. One small thing I'd love to see happen is for the birth certificate process to be more transparent. When our adoption was finalized, the girls were issued completely new birth certificates with our names in place of their first parents' names. This is an unnecessary and frankly immoral choice that has harmed adoptees who have searched for information about their history for years. As we learn to navigate adoption in a way that centers adoptees more, amending this process to reflect a reality that does not erase part of their identity would be an objective first step.

When my fostering friends and I talk about what we'd love to see change in the world of foster care, there is no end to theoretical suggestions, but like most systems that need to be overhauled, we often feel like we don't know where to start. When I get overwhelmed, I ask myself the same question I did when I was actively fostering: what actually benefits the child?

In my time as a foster parent, I've seen a lot of progress made in helping foster families have the resources they need to continue providing for kids in care. I've also seen some positive movement for older kids who are aging out of care. While both of these things are important and good, they are stopgap measures put in place at the end of a problem cycle. We really need to wrestle more with how to address the issues on the front end of the cycle. I know that change is slow and incremental, and I appreciate that these problems are multi-faceted and look different from state to state and county to county. I applaud those working to improve outcomes in communities regarding poverty, addiction, mental health, educational disparities, and communal trauma.

All of these mammoth issues are complex moving targets that contribute to why kids come into care.

The middle of the problem is the most ambiguous: how do we improve the process for kids in care? We can start with changing and enforcing laws that protect them. We can train all parties involved in trauma-informed care. We can reframe this discussion as one that affects the entire community. Because it does. There are hundreds of thousands of kids in care across the United States at any given time. We are all affected by foster care, and we have to keep talking about it like our lives depend on it.

Since finishing the original manuscript of this book in 2019, a lifetime has passed. Enough has happened to fill the pages of another book. We continue to communicate with our girls' first family. After living in Washington for two years, our family moved to Virginia. Our travels have taken us through southern Illinois with some regularity, and we've been able to get together for meals with Don and his extended family and with Jessica's parents. Don's mom, the one who told me point blank the first time I met her that she wanted us to adopt the girls, sends gifts for Christmas every year. We have not yet been able to see Jessica or Chad again, but I hope one day I will.

One of the greatest gifts of this process for me continues to be my relationship with Kelly. She and her husband, Aaron, adopted K shortly after our adoption was finalized. Their foster care license is still open, and Kelly runs a camp every summer for kids in care. Following Bea, Case, K, and S (who lived with Jessica for a full year before being brought into care), four more siblings have been added to the family. S and the next two were adopted by Teagan and Adam, a couple who found out about our family through case workers and other small world connections. The last two kids are currently in care with Amber and Charlie, experienced foster parents who have known Teagan and Adam for years.

As this part of the story continues to unfold, I remain steadfast in my commitment to staying connected with our girls' biological siblings.

With the addition of each new foster/adoptive family, we've invited them into what is affectionately referred to as the Foster Mafia. I had the same conversation with Teagan and then Amber that I did all those years ago with Kelly in the booth at Panera: this is weird and not ideal, but I'd love to be allowed to be a part of your life for the sake of our kids. With time, I've shared why I think it's important that they all have some kind of connection with our now eight kids' first family members. Each of us has had to discern what that looks like for ourselves, but the general philosophy is the same for all of us: we're family.

Kelly, Teagan, Amber, and I communicate almost daily. We compare medical charts when needed, and we marvel at the similarities in children who are biologically connected but being raised in different homes. They all live close to each other and see each other regularly. When someone has a sick kid, the others drop off meals or cover daycare pick-ups for the other kids. When we travel through the area, we try our best to get together with anyone who can meet up, and I hope one day we'll live closer and be a part of the everyday mundane with them.

Our family closed our license for now to focus on a lot of competing priorities. It was the right move to give me the space to focus on advocating for our girls' health and educational needs, which often feels like a full-time job. This decision also gave me the space to dust off this manuscript at the right time.

I'm open to fostering again because even though it's the hardest good thing I've ever attempted in my life, fostering is also something that feels like my comfort zone at this point. If we never open our license again, I can be at peace with trying to affect change informed by our experience, and I'll carry the lessons learned into the future.

Last Christmas, the girls asked for room makeovers. They have shared a room from the beginning, and I didn't know how designing these spaces for them would bring up all kinds of feelings for me. When they came to live with us, we set up a functional, generic baby/

toddler-friendly room in our house. All the colors were cute but neutral. We had supplies to serve a range of ages.

When it became clear they would be staying with us for a long time (but with no permanency in sight), I made each of them some magnet letters to hang their names on white boards above their beds. It was something personal, but also something that could easily be swapped out for another kid if they left us. It's wild to think about how long my heart had to live in that space even though it belonged fully to them.

Their new rooms—an ocean theme for Bea and a Barbie theme for Case—are representative of both of these girls. Case's is all play and bright colors and nooks for tinkering. Bea's is a calm oasis reminiscent of her favorite place where she can relax and center.

Doing this for them means so much more than I knew it was going to. It's a gift that I didn't give them as babies like I did the boys, but one that feels like a perfect metaphor for what adoption is like so much of the time—wonky timing and imperfect execution but a collaborative process where they take the lead, and I try to order their world in the way that best accommodates them.

One of the phrases we've taken to using with the kids is, "Go be your favorite self!" Because of our time working in foster care, my favorite self is the one who now focuses on building community, leading with empathy, and pursuing creative solutions in all I say and do.

RESOURCES

Here is a list of books mentioned throughout this story. I have found one of the greatest tools for combatting both unjust systems and my anxiety is educating myself as much as possible. These are just a few titles that helped me work through the challenges I described.

- *The Connected Child* by Dr. Karyn Purvis
- *Falling Free* by Shannan Martin
- *Trauma Stewardship* by Laura van Dernoot Lipsky
- *All You Can Ever Know* by Nicole Chung
- *Extremely Loud and Incredibly Close* by Jonathan Safran Foer
- *Beloved Chaos* by Jamie Zumwalt
- *Brave Souls: Experiencing the Audacious Power of Empathy* by Belinda Bauman

ACKNOWLEDGEMENTS

First, I have to thank Katie Otey, without whom this book would not exist. No one wanted to publish a book about foster care by an unknown author with too small a social media following, so I put it away, reasoning with myself that at least it served the purpose of being a work of personal catharsis. You were one of the first and last readers, providing insight and motivation for me to make this the best book it could be. You have consistently been my champion in professional and personal ways, and you are one of the greatest gifts in my life. I'm tempted to make a won't he do it joke here, but this is no laughing matter. You're the real MVP.

Thank you to all my readers who are intensely, extravagantly supportive of me without fail. You have been telling me to publish a book like this for 20+ years—ever since I was emailing from a ship off the coast of Sierra Leone. If you like this book, I'll write another one. If you don't, I will never know because you're the biggest hype squad in the world. Thank you for always filling my cup to overflowing.

Thank you to Jamie, Tamra, and April for your keen insights in the editing stages. Thank you too, April, for giving me the gift of Marcel's artwork in creating this perfect cover. And thank you, Marcel, for being one of the smartest, most inspiring little kids I've ever had the pleasure of knowing via your parents' social media accounts. Your future in … anything you want to do … is as bright as your beautiful artwork.

Thank you, Larry, for swooping in to save the day with all your design skills. I have loved working with you every step of the way.

To Scott, thank you for always encouraging me to turn my good ideas into action and for partnering with me to raise the four best kids on the planet. Or at least the block. Most definitely in our house.

Thank you to my parents, Steve and Nancy Hollingsworth, whose consistency and dedication to both raising me to be a decent human and cheering me on as a creator is parallel to none. Everything I am starts with you, and I will never take for granted the foundation you laid in my childhood of love, generosity, and commitment. I love well because you loved me well first.

To Will, Ben, Bea, and Case. I've had a lot of jobs in my lifetime, and my favorite one is being your mom. The four of you—my rain-cloud, my rain, my rainbow, and my morning dew—are my most eager and deliberate teachers. You are my favorite people, and wherever we are together is my favorite place. Thank you for letting me tell stories about your lives from the perspective of living mine. I am endlessly fascinated by and in awe of you. I love you for exactly who you are, and that will never change. Please put your clean clothes away, and bring the baskets back to the laundry room.

Printed in the USA
CPSIA information can be obtained
at www.ICGtesting.com
LVHW010415280824
789294LV00006B/151

9 781736 130360